Sir Lewis Morri

A vision of saints

By Lewis Morris

Sir Lewis Morri

A vision of saints
By Lewis Morris

ISBN/EAN: 9783337336349

Printed in Europe, USA, Canada, Australia, Japan

Cover: Foto ©Lupo / pixelio.de

More available books at **www.hansebooks.com**

BY
LEWIS MORRIS

FIDELIBUS
— — —

LONDON
KEGAN PAUL, TRENCH, TRÜBNER & CO., Lᴛᴅ
1890

PREFACE.

THE writer has carried out in the present poem the design which he had long entertained of attempting for the beautiful Christian legends and records that which has so often been done for the mythology of Greece.

It has been, as will be seen, his desire, not to confine himself to the Saints of any one Church or Creed, but to appeal to the spirit common to them all, which in all ages, and through every form of belief, has animated the whole company of faithful men.

PENBRYN,
October, 1890.

CONTENTS.

	PAGE
INTRODUCTION	1
THE SEVEN SLEEPERS OF EPHESUS ...	6
S. CHRISTOPHER	19
ANTONINUS PIUS ...	35
SS. PERPETUA AND FELICITAS ...	43
S. CECILIA	60
SS. ADRIAN AND NATALIA	69
S. PHOCAS	84
S. DOROTHEA	96
S. ALEXIS	107
S. MARINA	134
S. FRANCIS OF ASSISI	143
S. ELIZABETH OF HUNGARY ...	162
S. ROCH	184

	PAGE
S. Catharine of Siena	196
George Herbert	209
John Bunyan	222
Henry Martyn	240
Elizabeth Fry	256
Father Damien	271
Conclusion	289

A VISION OF SAINTS.

Once, long years since, I dreamt a dream of Greece
And fair fantastic tales of Nymph and Faun
And thin heroic forms, and ghostly gods
Floating in loveliness by grove and hill
And lake-side, all the joyous innocent grace
Of the old Pagan fancies; mixt with tales
Of passion and unhappy deeds of old,
Dark, unforgotten.
                Yesternight I knew
Another dream, a vision of old Rome,
Sterner and harsher, and the new-born grace
Of sacrifice; of life which for the Truth
Bore misery to the death, while they, the blithe
Faint gods of Fancy, sank to fiends of Ill

Athirst for pain and blood, and the old grace
To the new suffering, and the careless lives
That were content to enjoy, and asked no more
Than some brief glimpse of Beauty ere they died,
To grave bent brows, and tortured limbs, and all
The armoury of pain.

      And once again,
As the great Master passed from Hell to Heaven,
With an angelic guide, I seemed to tread
Where in the infinite Empyrean dwell
The blessed company of Saints, and move,
Conveyed by soaring wings to highest heaven,
'Midst those who bare of old the victor's palm
And wore the crown—martyr and eremite,
Lives spent in toil for God, or fired with love,
An infinite concourse pure and white as snow;
While far away on that unbounded air
Scarce reached by sight were saints of hoary eld,
Who by old Nile or the Chaldæan plain,

A Vision of Saints.

Through grave lives lighted by a certain hope,
Foreknew the weighing of the soul for doom,
And that unaided, darkling way which threads
The Valley of the Shadow, and passed to life
Dim centuries, ere yet the Lawgiver
Strode from the fiery Hill with face aflame,
Down to the listening Tribes.
      Not of old days
Were all the souls I saw, nor yet of Rome,
In birth or faith, but down long vistas gray
Of centuries we fared, by endless ranks
Of sanctity, cloistered or secular,
But all of Heaven; and later born in time,
Preachers inspired and ministering souls
Of women, whom no vow nor cell immured,
But a great pity drew and pious care
For fallen lives, and those who in the world,
Not of it—poets, thinkers, lawgivers,
Lovers of Country, of the Race, of God,

High souls and just who wrought in sight of all,
Toilers obscure who worked their work and died—
Bloom, in all time, the innumerable throng
That, year by year, the Eternal Seasons raise
To make our poor world sweet.
      All these I saw,
A concourse vast of every race and tribe
And tongue; till as I gazed, a shining band
New risen, and bearing on their front the mark
Of our quotidian life and modern speech,
Streamed through the boundless vast; and as we passed
These saints long risen, or mortal yesterday,
I questioned him who led me of the lives
And fate of some, and he, with solemn speech,
Made answer as we went.

      But ere we came
To real lives, lived upon earth for Heaven,
Two gracious legends, like the vanished tales
Of older Greece, twin dreams within my dream,

Each with its precious, hidden treasure, took
My eyes awhile, twin truths on which are built
Our newer, higher hope, but of old time
Unknown or dimly felt—the blessed dream
Which all have dreamt and shall, of life which ends not
With the last breath, but, to some finer air
Escaping, doth renew itself and fare
To what high work we know not, in some sphere
Unreached by thought, yet sure; and one the strength
Of weakness, when the too strong soul bows low
Before God's will, and doth exalt itself
Through self-surrender. These, the corner-stones
Of all our Faith, my guide, in parables
Part true, part feigned, declared to me, and I
Listened with eager ears.
      And first I seemed
To greet a joyous, radiant company,
Seven comely youths who, fresh from secular sleep,
From out a caverned hillside issued blithe
To meet the long-lost day. And thus my guide:

"When Rome was Pagan still, a little band
Of ardent, generous youths who called on Christ,
Fled their idolatrous city, thinking scorn
To kneel to those false gods their souls abhorred—
And loathing that accursèd heathen rout
Turned to the silence of the lonely hills
That brood round Ephesus, and found at length
Shelter and peace, within a winding cave
High on the rock-faced side of Cælian,
And there dwelt safe, lifting their gracious hymns
In worship to the Lord.
                        At last there came
Some heathen passer-by, who heard the sound,
And straight betrayed them. And the tyrant sent

His soldiers, and that none came forth again
Rolled in the narrow entrance monstrous rocks,
Which shut out air and light.   Then when they knew
No change of night and day, and all their food
Had failed, came Heaven-sent sleep to close their eyes.
Deep sleep which knew no waking fell on them
For the long space of nigh two hundred years.

There they slept on till now the conquering Cross
Bare sway, and 'twas a Christian Cæsar ruled
Where raged the Pagan erst.   For thirty years
The pious Theodosius swayed the might
Of Rome, and then the powers of evil bred
Dark heresies to rend the seamless robe
The Pagan might not.   Doubting voices cried,
'No resurrection is there, but the body
Lies rotting in the earth, and the freed soul
Weltering upon the unbounded seas of space
Is lost within the Universe, nor more

Takes its old shape. What? did the prophets know,
Moses, Esaias, and the rest, this thing?
There is no place of souls nor judgment day
Of deeds done in the flesh, nor heaven nor hell,
Only upon the earth our kingdom is.
Be wise and occupy, for never indeed
Comes any resurrection of the dead;
The dead are gone, cleave to the living alone;
Use all your nature. Lives the flower again,
The brute that comes so near us, and is full
Of faithful love and reverence for man
As man for God? If all these die and pass,
Then shall not we? What else than arrogant pride
Blinds men to fact, and fools them with a world
No eye has seen, which all the seers of old
Knew not nor proved? Nay, surely it were well
To take our lives in our own hands, and tread
Our fearless paths not looking for reward
To any dim unreal sphere, but deem

Our individual life ends with the grave,
As ends the flower in frost ; or if there come
Something of higher life, yet 'tis the Race
Which profits, nought beside.   Wherefore in vain
Are all your hopes of heaven, your fears of hell,
Since 'tis not men who live again, but Man.'

Thus having heard, the pious Cæsar turned,
Struck cold with doubt, as one a palsy takes,
Making his limbs hang impotent, his will
Powerless to live or die.   Alone he sate,
Hating the voice, hating his doubt, himself
Who doubted, and long time from sight of men
Withdrew himself and, clad in sackcloth, pined
With ashes on his head, yet found not peace
For all his penance, but the spectral doubt
Weighed on him like a nightmare night and day.

Now at the selfsame hour, when Cæsar strove
With his immense despair, a humble hind,

Seeking to find a shelter for his flock,
Chanced on the secret cave of Cælian,
And toiling with his fellows rolled aside
The rocks which sealed its mouth, and went his way,
Nor entered; but when now, returning dawn
Flooded the long-sealed vault with cheerful day,
It pierced to where the sleepers lay, and breathed
Some stir of coming life, and they once more
Drinking the brisk sweet breath of early morn
Opened their long-closed eyes, and woke again
To the old earth, and kept the far off past
Unchanged in memory, and spake with mirth
Of their long sleep, and the fair dreams it brought,
And said a prayer, and sang a hymn, and then,
Urged by the healthy zest of vigorous youth,
Sent one among them, Malchus hight, to buy
Food for their hunger.
                    Fearfully he stole
Down the long steep to where great Ephesus

The Seven Sleepers of Ephesus.

Shining beneath him lay. Scant change was there,
Only the stately house of Artemis
He found not where it stood. Half dazed he seemed
By too long sleep. But when he gained the gate
Of the city, on the walls behold the Cross!
The witness to the faith by which he lived,
The blessed symbol, which to own was death!
But still he seemed to dream, and wondering sought
Another gate, and there again the Cross!
And as he mused what portent 'twas he saw
The passers freely named the holy name
Which yesternight brought doom. Then with great joy,
Yet deep perplexity, he turned to greet
Some face he seemed to know, but it was strange,
And strange the fashion of the dress, and strange
The accent of the tongue, till, half afraid,
Entering where bread was bought, and offering gold,
The seller looking saw an ancient coin
Of Decius, and would ask him whence it came,

Deeming he found by some unhallowed spell
Forbidden treasure, and the youth's strange garb
And speech, and great perplexity, enforced
The doubt, so that they bound him fast and haled him
Through the long streets, where all in vain he sought
One friendly glance, to where upon his throne
The Bishop judged; and when the agèd man
Questioned him of the thing, and what had been,
And sware him on the Cross, straightway the youth—
' We fled the tyrant Decius, who would bid us
Serve the false gods, and—was it yesternight?—
Rolled ponderous rocks to seal the cave where I
And my companions slept; but now, I pray you
What is it that has been?   Bear you the Cross
And fear not?   Call men now upon the name
Of Christ and dread not all the bitter pains—
The dungeon, and the torture, and the stake,
The tyrannies our fathers knew and we?
What change is this assails my ears and eyes—

Strange speech, strange vestments, forms and faces strange?
Where is the shining house of Artemis?
I pray you tell me what it is has been,
And whether I be alive or long time dead,
Deceived in dreams by long unnoted years.'

Then fell the Bishop, full of pious awe,
Prostrate at Malchus' feet—the agèd man
Before the spirit clothed with changeless youth,
Since well he knew what thing his eyes had seen—
A miracle of life, raised from the grave,
A miracle of Heaven.   And all the throng,
Bishop and governor, with all the great
And noble of the city, white-haired lords,
And stately matrons, coming, knelt with him
Before the youth, o'er whose unwrinkled brow
Two hundred years had passed and left no sign—
Swift-coming age before eternal youth,
Brief life before the endless life of death.

Then went they forth, that noble throng, and all
The city, to where upon the Cælian hill
The seven youthful martyrs lay so long.
There in the cave, the blessed company
Sate cheerful, wondering much to see the throng,
With Malchus leading them; and as the array
Drew nearer, heard the sound of hymns, and saw
The sacred symbol borne on high, and knew
All that had been, and that the might of Wrong
Was broken, and the world was of the Faith,
And the false gods no more; and then they raised
Their clear accordant strains in praise to heaven,
And from their happy heads crowned round with light,
And from their cheeks red with the heavenly rose,
And from their lips touched with divinest song,
An effluent glory shone, and all who saw
Knew that their eyes beheld the blessed dead.

Last, Theodosius wrestling with his doubt,
And almost conquering, sped o'er land and sea
To see the portent, and when he was come
And stood before the place the Pagan erst
Sealed fast with monstrous rocks, on the young lives
Fresh vowed to Christ, and left them there to die,
He knelt in silence, and the fire of faith
Burned high in him, and dried the deeps of doubt.
And when he looked on those immortal eyes,
And that first bloom of an immortal youth,
His faith grew perfect, and he blest the Lord
Who sent the sign.   Then, with one voice sublime,
The seven awakened spirits sang, 'Believe,
Believe through us, O Cæsar!   We are dead,
And yet we live.   Praise Heaven that we have seen
The faith triumphant.   Ere the last great day
The Lord has raised us that men should be strong,
And doubt no longer, but believe indeed

'The life and resurrection of the world.'

And when their voices died away they bowed
Their heads upon their breasts, and kneeling, gave
Their spirits back to God; and all who saw,
And all who heard, Cæsar, and all the throng,
Doubted no more, but rose and did believe."

Which things, when I had heard, again I seemed
To hear my guide, " Know, thou that hearest me,
Through the round world this fair old legend runs
Where man is higher than the beasts that die.
The Hindu, dreaming on his seething plains,
Cherishes it; the fierce false prophet stole
The story; and throughout the fabulous East
It lives and thrives to-day; the frozen North
Holds it for true; o'er all the ancient world
Some fair faint blossom of the gracious tale

Lingers, and in the modern springs anew
In witness to the light-winged hours which snatch
The swift unconscious life from youth to age.
Too fair, too fleeting, change confusing change—
Change of a day which works the work of years;
Unchanging years, which seem but as a day!"

" But with still clearer voice, and sweeter tongue,
Thus speaks the legend: 'Sleep and Death are one,
Not diverse, and to Death's long slumber comes
Awakening sure and certain, when the Dawn
Of the Last Day shall break, and shall unseal
The long-closed eyes, as that strong sun of Spring
Illumed the caves of sleep, and stirred the blood
Which else had slumbered still.' Yet since no sign
Comes from our sleepers here, the yearning hearts
Which mark the struggling breath come short and faint,
The tired eyes close, and the calm peace which smooths
The weary brow—and feel 'tis sleep—no more—

Yet find no proof, cherish the legend fair,
Because life longs to be, because to cease
Is terrible, because the listening soul
Waits for some whisper from beyond the grave,
Waits still, as it has waited through all time,
Waits undismayed, whate'er its form of creed,
Nor fails, though all is silence, to hold fast,
Deep in its sacred depths, too deep for thought,
The Resurrection and the Life to be."

S. Christopher.

Next 'twas a tall and stalwart form I saw,
Like Herakles of old, who strode along,
Bearing a staff which seemed to bud and bloom
Into the martyr's palm.   Fainter he showed
In outline than the rest, as if I saw
A veilèd life half hid behind a cloud
Of legend, or a real life, perhaps,
Set round with precious gems of allegory
And consecration fashioned from the sum
Of meaner lives, less sinful, less cast down,
And less triumphant.   Was it parable,
Not fact, that bid him be?   Then it was well
To feign the tale—the wave of death, the power

Of evil, the strong man who turned to good,
Whose fleshly strength was broken by the weight
Of a little child—and this dim saint, the thrall
Of evil once, is precious, as the lives
We track from birth to death.
                    Thus then my guide
Held converse as we passed.
                    "No name there is
More strange and quaint and sweet than Christopher's,
Who bore the Christ.
                    In the far fabulous East
He served, a soldier. Nature, which so oft
Grudges her gifts, gave this man strenuous limbs
And giant strength, joined with the choicer gift
Of a keen brain, and daring will, and high
Ambition which aspires. Him the clear voice
Of high adventure called o'er land and sea,
The magical music, heard of nobler souls,
Which dulls all lower voices. More than Prince

S. Christopher.

This strenuous champion showed, a King of men,
Who saw Power shining starlike on the hills
And set his face to reach it.   Luxury
Held him nor sensual ease, who was too great
For silken fetters ; a strong will and arm
Bent to a higher end than those, and fired
By higher longings.
     Every soul of man
Knows its own weakness, so this strength o'ergrown
Only achievement drew.   O'er land and sea,
From realm to realm, he fared, seeking a Lord
Still mightier than the last, until at length
A slumbering soul, not prizing good or ill,
He found a puissant Prince and served content.

But 'mid the rugged ways of this sad world,
As now he fared unmoved, the frequent sight
Of evil; the blind rage which takes and sways
The warrior in the fight; the hopeless pain

Which unregarded cries to Heaven; the wrong
Done on the earth for ever; the great sum
And mystery of Evil, worked on him
With that strange spell of power which only takes
The strong soul captive.   Here was strength indeed,
Greater than mortal, which had power to bind
The mightiest in chains, now forcing them
Despite themselves to wrong, now binding them
With sensual fetters.   Was not this enough
To limit Heaven itself?   So this rude soul
Bowed to it, taking Evil for his god,
A voluntary thrall.   Yet not to him
The smooth foul ways of sense, the paths of wrong,
Brought pleasure of themselves; only a beat
Of pulsing life, the keenness and the glow
Of full impassioned being.   So long time
He served the Lord of Evil; deeds of wrong
And anger knew he, stains of sensual sin;
So that, for dread of him, men named his name

'The Unrighteous,' but he recked not.   Power and fame
Sufficed him long, and hid from him the fashion
Of his own life, and by what perilous ways
He went, and black unfathomed gulfs of Ill.

Till one day, as he journeyed (so the tale,
The allegory of this sinful soul)
Through a thick wood, which was the deadly shade
Of sense, and of the world, which hid the heavens,
Blinding the eye of day ; with wondering thought
He knew his vanquisher, the Lord of Ill,
Cower down as from a blow, hiding his eyes
From some white suffering form.
                                            And lo ! his gaze
Met that great symbol of all sacrifice
Which men have worshipped since ; the soft sad eyes,
The painful limbs fixed to the Tree of Death
Which is the Tree of Life ; and all the past
Fell from him, and the mystery of Love

And Death and Evil; Might which gives itself
To save the Race, and dying, breaks in twain
The vanquished strength of Hell; all these transformed
His inmost being, and his prisoned soul,
Spurning its former chain, stood fair and free,
Unfettered, for a while, and then he fell
Prone on the earth, the mild and pitying eyes
Bent on him still.   There he lay motionless
A night of precious sorrow, till at last
The sun rose on the earth and on his soul,
And Dawn, returning, brought the purer Day.

But when he rose the ancient mastery
And thirst for power, springing anew in him
Once more resistless, over land and sea
Drave him to seek this new and mightier Lord
Who brake the power of Ill.   So far and wide
He fared, a passionate Pilgrim, but found not
The Lord Divine—for Him indeed his eyes

Saw not as yet—filled with the pride of life,
Touched with desire for good, since it was strong,
But prizing strength alone.
                    Till as he fared
His footsteps chanced upon a stony land
Where sprang no herb. There, in a lonely cell,
Pondered an aged man; no other thing
Of life was there, only wan age, which paused
Upon the verge of death. His giant strength
Was flagging now. Beyond the ghostly hills
The sun was sinking, and the gray of night
Stole upward. Through the plain beneath the cell
A broad black river raged, spanned by no bridge
For travellers, but a dark road stole to it
O'ergloomed by cypress, and no raft was there
Nor ferry. Evermore beyond the shade,
Breast-high, the strong stream roared by dark as doom.

There on the brink he paused, and saw no soul,

Watching the stream of death.   Great misery
And weakness took him, and he sank, o'erborne,
Prone on the strand.   Then on the farther shore
The sunset, glancing for a moment, fired
A thousand palace casements, soaring spires,
And airy domes, and straight his glad soul knew
That he had seen the city of the King.

Then presently he heard a reverend voice
From out the gloom.   And now the sun had set,
And all the hills were hidden.
                              'Son, thou com'st
Seeking the Lord of Life.   There is no way
But through yon cruel river.   Thou wert strong:
Take rest and thought till strength return to thee.
Arise, the Dawn is nigh.'
                         Then they twain went,
And there that faint soul rested many days.

S. Christopher.

But when the strong man's strength was come again
His old guide led him forth to where the road
Sank in that dark swift stream. The hills were veiled;
There was no city to see, nought but thick cloud,
And still that black flood roaring. Then he heard
The old voice whisper, ' Not of strength alone
Come they who find the Master, but cast down
And weak and wandering. Yet since strength indeed
Well used is precious, therefore shalt thou plunge
In yon cold stream. Death shall not come to thee,
Nor in those chill dark waters shall thy feet
Slip, nor thy life be swallowed. Be it thine
To bear in thy strong arms the fainting souls
Of pilgrims who pass onward day and night,
Seeking the Lord of Light. Thou who long time
Didst serve the Lord of Evil now shalt serve
A higher; and because great penances
Are fitting for great wrong, here shalt thou toil

Long years, till haply thou shalt lose the stain
Of sense and of the world; then shall thy eyes
See that thou wouldst. Go, suffer and be strong.'

'Then that rude soul, treading those stony ways,
Went down into the waters. Piteous cries
Called loud to him for help, poor wayfarers
Come to life's goal; wan age and budding youth,
And childhood fallen untimely. He stooped down
With wonder mixed with pity, solacing
Those weakling limbs, and, bearing in his arms
The helpless burden, through the chill dark depths
Of those black swirling waters, undismayed,
Strode onward. Oftentimes the deadly chill
Of ice-cold floods too strong for feebler hearts
Assailed him, yet his giant stature still
Strode upright through the deep to the far shore.
And those poor pilgrims with reviving souls
Blessed him, and left the waters, and grew white

And glorified, and in their eyes he knew
A wonder and a rapture as they saw
The palace of the King, the domes, the spires,
The shining oriels sunlit into gold,
The white forms on the verge to welcome them,
And the clear heights, and the discovered heaven.

But never on his eyes, for all his toil,
Broke that clear sun, nor those fair palace roofs,
As erst upon his weakness. Day and night
He laboured unrewarded, with no gleam
Of that eternal glory, which would shine
Upon those fainting souls, whom his strong arms
Bare upward. Day and night he toiled alone
Amid the deeps of death. Oft would he rise
At midnight, when the cry of sinking lives
Called to him on the brink, and succour them
Without a thought of fear. Yea, though the floods
Roared horribly, and deep called unto deep,

Straight through those hidden depths he strode unmoved
A strong, laborious, unrewarded soul.

Was it because the blot of former sin
Clung to him still uncleansed? I cannot tell;
The stain of ill eats deep. But to my thought
Not thus the legend runs; rather, I deem
He loved in good the strength which erst enthralled
His life to ill. Therefore this striving soul
Still laboured unfulfilled.
     Thus the slow years
Passed, till the giant strength at times would flag
A little, and yet bore on. But one still night,
Ere cockcrow, when the world was sunk in sleep,
A summons came; and he arising saw,
With some strange new compassion, on the brink
A childish form. A sweet sad glance divine
Shone from the eyes. And as the strong man took
The weakling to his heart, through the great power

Of Pity with new strength, he braved the deep
Careless with that light load.
                        But in mid stream
The more than human force, the dauntless spirit
Which long time bore unfalt'ring the great load
Of mortal ills—ay, though the loud winds beat
And the thick night was blind—these failed him now,
And, as by some o'erwhelming weight opprest,
His flagging forces tottered; the cold wave
Rose high around him; the once haughty head
Bowed low, the waters stealing to his lip
Engulfed; the burden of the painful world
Crushed his weak shoulders; and a bitter cry
Burst from him—' Help! I faint, I sink, I die,
I perish; I am spent, and can no more.
My strength is naught, the deep floods swallow me.
Not of myself I conquered, but of Thee.'

Then suddenly from his spent life he knew

The load withdrawn, and through the midnight gloom
There burst the glorious vision of his dreams,
The palace of the King, the domes, the spires,
The shining oriels sunlit into gold,
The heaven of heavens discovered, and a voice—
' Thou hast sustained the whole world, bearing Me
The Lord of Earth and Heaven. Rise; turn awhile
To the old shore of Time. I am the King
Thou seekest. I have known thy sin, thy pain,
Thy tears, thy penitence. If thy soul ask
Proof of these things, this sign I give to thee.
Set thou thy staff to-night upon the verge
Of these dark waters, and with break of dawn
Seek it, and thou shalt find it burgeon forth
With fair white scented blossoms. This shall be
Witness of what has been.'
      And he with joy,
Vanquished at length, obeyed, and with the dawn
Where stood his staff, there sprang the perfumed cup

And petals of a lily: so the tale.
Nay, but it was the rude strength of his life
Which blossomed into purity, and sprang
Into a higher self, beneath the gaze
Of a little child.—Nay, but it was the might
Of conscious strength, which cast its robes of price
Down on the earth; the new self stripped and purged
Of ingrained pride, which from the deeps of death
Rose painful to the stable earth again,
And grew regenerate through humility.

So for the remnant of his days he served
The Lord of Good, a champion of the Right,
Grown meek. At last the Pagan governor
Bade him deny the Lord who succoured him;
Whom he contemning, gained a martyr's crown
Through pain and death, and is Saint Christopher."

He ended, and I mused in silent thought

On this quaint legend, when again my guide—
" Even so they toil as he, the striving souls
Who live on earth to-day engrossed with care
Willing to better our poor world, which calls
Always with piteous suffrages to Heaven—
Strong souls with deep compassion for the race,
Seeming possest, yet vainly, since their labour
Born of the half unconscious pride of strength
Is only part for others, or for God.
But when a nobler, self-less passion fills
The heart and soul, then only fit reward
Is theirs, and from the depths of their dead selves,
And from the staff of their discarded strength,
And from the unneeded treasures of their past,
The yearning to fulfil the Perfect Scheme,
The full surrender to the Heavenly Will,
Obedience, self-effacement, sacrifice,
Life a white perfumed blossom springs to Heaven."

Antoninus Pius.

And as we left the haunted border-land
Of fantasy, for lives, which lived and died
In the long-vanished centuries, true indeed
Though broidered here and there with flowers of gold
By pious hands devouter than our own,
Yet mainly true; first of the endless line
I saw a calm and Princely Presence come,
Who, stately as the Imperial Purple, bore
His robe, a saint in mien, mild, innocent,
Perfect in manhood, with clear eye serene,
And lofty port; who from the sages took
What lessons earth could give, but trod no less
The toilsome path of Duty to the end;
And as he passed I knew the Kingly ghost

Of Antonine, who knew not Christ indeed
Yet not the less was His. I marked the calm
And thoughtful face of him who ruled himself,
And through himself the world, and 'mid the soil
And foulness of unfettered lusts kept pure
His virgin soul, and o'er the servile crowd,
Trembling, betrayed, beneath the armèd heels
Of a long line of tyrants trodden in blood,
Wielding a blameless sceptre, stayed awhile
By a white life, and perfect, lived for good
The hurrying doom and ruin of the world.

Whom when we passed, thus spake my heavenly guide :
"There are of Him, who call not on His name,
And this is of them, the best flower and fruit
Of all the Heathen world, the Sage who ruled
The race of men, for whom the fatal gift
Of power unfettered worked nor hurt nor harm,
But left his soul unchanged : for whom the gross

And sensual lusts which wrecked the hapless line
Of Cæsars were as nought, the coward fears
Of tyranny unknown, the secret arts
Of the informer hateful ; but he lived
The foremost citizen of Rome—no more
Nor lower, happy, loving wife and child
And all his people as a father might
The offspring of his love.   Then first indeed
Crowned, on a throne, Divine Philosophy
Swayed all the race of men, like that fair dream
Of the Athenian sage, and too great weal
Lulled them to sleep, till they forgot to prize
Their freedom lost for ever.   All his soul
Was filled with love of peace, holding it more
To save a single citizen than slay
A thousand enemies.   A thrifty hand
Grudging his people's toil, not less he planned
Great works and beautiful, which might enrich
The City of the world, and, loving peace,

Yet not the less the reverence for his name
Spread to earth's limits.   On the distant bank
Of Phasis, to a king whom Cæsar named,
The stubborn tribesmen bowed.   The Parthian spared
Armenia at his nod.   The Scythian hosts
On the Cimmerian shore confessed his might,
And on the wild Sarmatian plains his word
Was law, and many a barbarous chieftain came
To kneel his vassal, whom with soothing words
He would dismiss, deeming his load of rule
Sufficient without more.   For that great gift
Of Rome to men, just laws and wise, his thought
Devised new gains, filled with the purest love
Of Heaven-sent equity; and that rare flower
Of tolerance which best of all adorns
The philosophic brow, which those who call
On a Diviner name learn last of all,
Which wise Aurelius knew not, nor the books
Of all the sages taught, in this pure heart

Sprang up self-sown, and bloomed in noble deeds,
From sceptic Greek and unbelieving Jew,
Shielding the faith of Christ, not carelessly,
With that contemptuous charity the fruit
Of cold and doubtful minds, but born of trust
In the old faith, and therefore generous.

Dost wonder that against so white a soul,
So pure, so innocent, so rich in love,
There burned the causeless enmity that fires
The traitor's base ambition? Two there were;
But one the Senate doomed, the other fell
By his own hand. But when they told the saint,
Seeking to unmask some deep conspiracy,
He would not. 'Sure,' he said, ''twere little gain
To learn that of the people of my love
So many hate me.' Ah, fair words and high
Of one who spotless filled the blood-stained throne
Round which for two long centuries had twined

Rank growths of vile mistrust and hate and blood!

Thus through his long and peaceful years the saint
Lived cheerful. All good things were his to hold,
And hardly clouded days, because his soul
Took willingly his lot. And yet he lost
His well-loved sons before their budding age
Had come to flower. And yet 'twas his to bear
The curse of a vile woman; but his faith,
Greater than her offence, forbade him still
To hold her false; too pure, too meek a soul
To mate with such, or haply half aware
And yet forgiving all, like Him who bade
The sinner sin no more. Still on his life
The Sun of Righteousness shone clear and lit
His way with gleams of Heaven, and all his days
Were gilded, year by year, until the end,
As his who treads the duteous paths of life
And is content.

　　　　Then, when he came to die,
Commending, with calm love, his only child
And, most of all, the Empire which he loved
To him who followed him, the sage his hand
Had trained in his own virtues, tranquilly
He laid him on his bed ; and when the end
Drew near, the watchers heard the failing voice
Wander in dreams, and whisper of the State
And all his hopes for her.　And when he woke,
Laying all signs of sovereignty aside,
He bade them take the golden Victory,
The solemn symbol of Imperial power,
And bear it to Aurelius.　Last, when now
Life's tide was ebbing fast, he summoned to him
The tribune of the guard, and uttered clear,
As should an Emperor who led his hosts
To battle with the evil of the world,
The password of the day—one word, no more,
Calm and Imperial—' Æquanimitas.' "

And something in me seemed to rise and break
In utterance, and as we passed I cried,
"This man was of Thy name, O Lord, and Thou,
Among the ranks of those who lived ere yet
Thou camest, or called not on Thee, having come,
Didst never leave Thyself, or then or since,
Wholly without a witness, but didst set
Thy light for all to see, these precious blooms
Of purity, these priceless lives unstained
And spent for Duty, 'mid the strifes, the lusts
Of a polluted world."

And then I saw
Two girlish mothers, bearing each a child
Clasped to her breast, one with the conscious pride
Of noble birth, and one a lowlier form,
Who to the other looked with loving eyes
In which the old respect was mingled now
With a new sense of equal sisterhood;
And both with rapt gaze went, as keeping still
Some memory of surprise, since first they rose
From earth to heaven; and my guide named their names
Discoursing thus:
    " By the Tyrrhenian Sea
In Africa, when nigh two hundred years
Passed since Christ died, there lived a youthful wife,

Bearing her first-born infant at her breast,
Perpetua, of noble lineage, nursed
Safe in the shelter of her happy home
From maidenhood to gracious motherhood;
Nor broke there on her careless hours a sound
Of the great suffering of the painful world,
But evermore in gracious liturgies
Of homely life she spent her careless days,
Shielded from every breath of ruder air
Which might assault her, fenced about secure
By walls of love; sire, mother, brother, spouse,
Linking close arms around her, and her birth
And name, and rank and wealth, and honour of men
Made this rude path of life and rugged steep
Show, like the fields of June, a maze of flowers.

Now on those calm and slumbering days there burst
The New Faith like a flame, and the quick soul
Of the young wife was fired, and she became

A catechumen holding fast the truth,
Scorning the Pagan gods; and her young brother,
Like her, believed, and so in piety
They lived, till came an overwhelming wave
Of bloodshed once again, and they denounced
The faithful pair, and first Perpetua.

But when this great blow fell on him, her sire,
A noble, holding fast the faith of old
And loving with a father's love his girl
And her young child, ere yet the shadow of doom
Fell on them, went to her, and of his love
Would seek to bend her, using all the strength
Which venerable age and filial awe
Might give him; bade her pause awhile and seek
Counsel of wiser heads than hers, who knew
The riddles of the Faith, and what deep truths,
Though hid by myth, maybe, and parable,
The Pagan forms concealed. But she, with clear

Undoubting faith : 'My father, canst thou change
The fashion of a vessel, giving it
Another name?' And he : 'Nay, 'twere the same
Howe'er men called it.' Then she answered straight,
With fearless voice, 'Nor canst thou change my soul,
Which bears the name of Christ.' Then with deep grief
The old man raised his hand as if to strike,
But could not, seeing her undaunted soul,
And went his way, nor troubled her ; and she,
In that short time of rest, cleansing her soul
With the baptismal waters, rose refreshed,
A Christian, strong to suffer and give praise.

Then in a few brief days began the tale
Of Martyrdom. 'Tis her own voice that speaks
The story of her suffering. 'In the gloom
Of a dark prison cell, where stifling heat
And the rude insults of the brutal guard
Tortured each sense, I lay in misery.

SS. *Perpetua and Felicitas.*

There my young bondswoman Felicitas,
Wanting a month to labour, took with me
The sacred lustral waters, and we sate
Pining amid the squalor of the jail,
Until at last, their hard hearts moved by Heaven,
They brought my darling to me, and I gave him
Milk from my breast, and thenceforth day and night
I lived content, my child within my arms;
And those dull prison walls seemed more to me
Than my sire's palace, since I held my love
And kept my faith unchanged, and grew to be
Happier than ever in that careless life
Within my palace home.
      And then one day
My brother, who was partner in my bonds,
Seeing my cheerful and undaunted soul,
Spake thus to me: "Sister, I do perceive
Thou art Heaven's favourite; therefore to thy prayer
Doubtless the Lord will grant a blessèd dream,

Sent through the watches of the night, if thou
Wilt kneel to ask it, and we too shall know
Whether the martyr's crown is ours to wear
Or shameful freedom." Then I prayed, and, lo!
In the still watches of the night, a dream
Which showed a golden stairway to the skies.
Around it swords and hooks and all the array
Of martyrdom were ranged, and at its foot
A loathly monster, crouching, coil on coil,
To take the souls of those who fain would rise.
And when, with fear and trembling, I had passed,
Naming the sacred Name, to some blest place,
A garden, I ascended; there I saw
A shepherd with his flock around him ranged
By myriads on the grass, who welcomed me
And gave me of some mystic food, which I
Received with folded hands and took and ate.
And all the throng of saints, with one accord,
Pealed forth " Amen ; " and sudden I awoke,

SS. Perpetua and Felicitas.

Hearing their voices, and upon my lips
Lingered the sweetness of that heavenly food.
And when I told my brother of my dream,
We knew our hour was come, our fate assured,
And we with nothing more of fear nor hope.

Then after many days my father came,
Borne down with grief. " Daughter," he cried, " I pray
    thee,
Pity these scant gray hairs. If e'er thy sire
Loved thee beyond thy brethren, cherished thee
Through all thy childhood, watched thee till thou camest
To honourable wedlock, now, I pray thee,
Have pity on him; make him not the shame
Of all mankind. Or if indeed I fail,
With all my love, to bend thee, pity her,
Thy mother, who has borne thee, and who yearns
To clasp her child again. If none of these
Move thee, have pity on thy child, who pines

Without thee, nor can live without thy breast.
Nay, daughter, have compassion! See, thy father
Kneels to thee, lady, and in tears, and is
Thy suppliant for thyself!" But I, who knew
How wise he was and tender, felt my soul
Pierced through with sorrow. Yet the Faith! the Faith!
Should I betray it? "Nay," I said, "my father;
We all are in God's hand, who rules all things
Even as He will."
    Then sorrowful he went.

Now, when the day was come when we should stand
For trial of the Judge Hilarion,
Even as we stood before him, set on high
For all to see, when my turn came to plead,
Confessing Christ, I heard a cry, and lo!
My father with my infant in his arms,
Conjuring me with tender words of love
To spare him and my child, whom I had given

SS. *Perpetua and Felicitas.*

Life, and now doomed to death, recounting all
The misery I should bring. And my sweet turned
His darling eyes on me, and smiled and stretched
His little hands to me, and seemed to seek
His mother's breast. And the stern judge himself
Besought me to have mercy and to spare
My father and my child, and bade me burn
A little incense to the gods. But I,
Some new strength firing me, which swept away
The love of sire or child, made answer straight,
" I will not," and confessed I was of Christ.
And when my father strove to force me down
And hush my voice, the stern Hilarion
Gave word that they should scourge him; and I heard
The sound of blows, and felt my father's pain
Quiver through every nerve, and grew so faint
That he should suffer thus, and all for me,
Amid his honoured age, that scarce I marked
That cold voice dealing doom, the dreadful death

Of those the fierce brutes' tooth or claw or horn
Rends limb from limb.
                     And then they scourged with thongs
Our brother martyrs, while ourselves indeed,
Me and my bondswoman Felicitas,
They buffeted with blows upon the face.

But many visions, through the grace of Heaven,
Came to me ere the end, and on the eve
Of the great shows, when all day long my limbs,
Racked in the cruel stocks, scarce ceased to pain,
Amid the troubled thoughts of coming doom,
The hushed arena framed with cruel faces
Ready to gloat on death, the sudden roar
As from the darkling dens the famished beast
Leapt forth in fury, and the echoing cries
From the base coward throng reclining safe
To see their fellows bleed, there came a dream
Heaven-sent. For, lo! without the dungeon door

One seemed to knock; and when I opened to him,
The martyred saint, Pomponius, stood without,
Clad in white robes of brightness, all besprent
With pomegranates of gold.   One word he spake:
" Perpetua, we await thee."   And I followed,
And through dark ways he led me, till we came
Forth 'mid the still arena's sudden blaze.
And then he left me, and they bade me fight
No tiger, but some loathly shape of man,
Who held a bough laden with golden fruit
For prize of victory.   Then we strove long
Together; but I conquered, and I gained
The precious fruit, and suddenly I knew
That not with ravening tooth or rending claw
Alone 'twas mine to fight, but with the force
Of Evil, human-shaped, Evil without,
Evil within, if one would keep the Faith.'

Dear soul, so far she speaks, the rest for her

Is silence, but a witness speaks who saw
What things were done. When their last day was come,
On that accursèd Pagan holiday,
The people heard, thrilled with a shameful joy,
The roarings of the famished brutes beneath.
And they, too, heard it, and the gathering roar
Of the more brutal crowd; sitting alone
In silence and in darkness, till the hour
When they, weak nursing mothers, faithful youths,
Noble and slave, alike went forth to face
The oft imagined dread, the tooth, the claw,
The piercing horn, the spring, the devilish strength,
The same Hand fashioned which could frame the lamb.
Sure, 'twere no wonder if those delicate lives,
Forlorn of help, scorned, tortured, of their God
Forsaken, as their Master, had shrunk back
From that intolerable fear; but they
Shrunk not at all, strong souls, but dauntless went,
Leaving their new-born joys, and the young lips

Of children at the breast, home, love, young life,
And all for Christ, fronting the horrible dread
Unmoved, unfearing—went without a word
Through hollow stifling dungeons, lost in gloom,
To where, on a sudden, blazed the noonday glare
Above the arena, and the solitude
Horrid with pitiless eyes, and the loud roar
Of the imprisoned beasts behind the bars,
That presently the cruel spite of men
Should loose on them.
    And there they stood and sang
A hymn 'midst jeering thousands.　On the youth
Who suffered first, a leopard, springing, bathed
His poor frame in a baptism of blood;
And when, oh, shame! they stripped those wifely limbs
Before the ribald gaze of countless eyes—
They had not looked for that—a deadly chill
Took them, and what the terror of the beasts,
The lions' dreadful roaring, the fierce growl

Of the impatient tigers, the red jaws
Of the tall bears who shook their bars, the low
Fierce muttering of the bulls, whose lurid eyes
Glared on them, could not, wifely modesty
Had well-nigh done, when some new Heaven-sent shame
Touched the vile throng, who bade the jailers hide
Their nakedness; and there, in robes of white,
Naming the holy Name, they stood and took
The mad brutes' horrible rage, and, pierced and tost
By the sharp horn, and hurled in air, and trod
By the fierce rushing feet, they lay alone,
Bleeding upon the sand, swooning away,
Or by some heavenly ecstasy possessed
Which dulled their pain.

     But when Perpetua
Knew life return, she her dishevelled hair
Tied in a knot, and round her wounded limbs
Gathered her robe, and seeing on the ground
The young Felicitas, assuaged her pain

And lifted her, waiting again the rush
Of the fierce beast; but when he came no more,
The sordid crowd, still hungering for blood,
Demanded they should die before their eyes.

Then, in their midst, the dauntless martyr band
Stepped forth and gave the sacred kiss of peace,
And met swift death; but she, Perpetua,
From some unskilful hand or timorous, took
Repeated blows, and languished long, and bore
Wound upon cruel wound ere her pure spirit
Was freed and rose, and rested with the blest."

And straight my heart, hearing this piteous tale,
Was melted in me, and I seemed to cry,
"These are Thy saints, O Lord, like those whose bones
Lie scattered in Thy Alpine valleys cold,
Or who to-day by Thy idolatrous East,
Or Thy old Nile, or on the desert sands,

Or gemlike islets of the tropic sea,
Have died without a murmur for Thy sake.
Thou askest of Thy creatures sacrifice,
And it is given, nor yet with readier soul
In the first ages of the Faith than now.
Haply with blinder courage 'twas they went,
These protomartyrs, to their doom, than those
Who die to-day. With what high flame of faith
These souls were set on fire, who met unmoved—
Delicate lives lapt round with luxury—
The scorn of men, the jeering careless crowd,
The tortures of the fiends, rather than pay
False homage to false gods! And yet, indeed,
I know not if there be not sacrifice
As willing now; the Indian well to-day
Is choked with women's corpses, who had bought
Ease, wealth, and life, nay, more—the dearer lives
Of children—had they borne to bend the knee
To the false Prophet. Nay, Thy hand, O Lord,

Is strong as it was then, Thy seeming face
Averted as 'twas then, till the last breath
Sobs from the painful lips, and Thou dost bid them
Enter into Thy joy.   Thou seest all
And speakest not, but these Thy servants hear
Some still small whisper which the duller sense
Of the world may not take.   But whoso hears
Thy voice, for him the aspect of things seen
And felt—the world without, the world within—
The old familiar landmarks of his life,
The heavens, the earth, the sea, no longer show
As undetermined fantasies ; but all
The smiling summer plains, the storm-wrapt hills,
The clear cold dawn, the angry furious night,
Lives bright as Heaven, lives dark as nether Hell,
Joy, grief, pain, pleasure, mingle and are part
Of the unfolding mystery of Faith."

Then, as we passed, we came on one whose face
The whole world knows—so fine a soul and hand
Saw her long since, and fixed her for our eyes—
A maiden with rapt gaze, and at her side
An idle music; listening half entranced
To some celestial harmonies unheard
Save by pure souls like hers.   There was no need
To name her name, when thus the tale began :

" Once in old Rome, long centuries ago,
There lived a pair, noble in rank and soul,
Who, though the Pagan idols still bare sway,
Knelt not to them, holding the faith of Christ.
And one fair girl was theirs, Cecilia,

S. Cecilia.

Nourished on thoughts of virgin purity
Which filled her cloistered gaze.   No earthly love
Might touch her pure pale soul, which always viewed,
Lit only by the frosty moon of faith,
The cold clear peaks of soaring duty pierce
The still blue vault of heaven, as soar the snows
Of lifeless Alp on Alp, where comes no herb
Nor blade of green, but all the icy world
Dreams wrapt in robes of sterile purity.

For evermore to her rapt eyes the skies
Stood open, evermore to her rapt ear
Celestial music came, and strains unheard
By mortal ear amid the throng of life
Hushed all the lower tones and noise of earth
With heavenly harmonies; and the high notes
Of the angelic chanting seraphim
Would occupy her life, until her soul,
Rapt by the ravishing sound, would seem to 'scape

From her raised eyes, and float, and speed itself
Between the rhythmic wings of harmony,
Even to Heaven's gate, and was transformed and lost
Its earthly taint; and sometimes on her lips
Thin traces of the heavenly music dwelt,
Which bound the listener fast, and of her skill
Some half-remembered echoes, faint yet sweet,
Were born again on lute or pipe, and linked
The world with Heaven; the immortal chanting quires
With earth's poor song; the anthems of the blest
With our weak halting voices, till the being
Of that fair virginal interpreter,
Pierced with keen melodies, and folded round
With golden links of gracious harmonies,
Was all possest of Heaven, and to her thought
It seemed a guardian angel stood by her
In sleep or waking hours, so that no care
For earth or earthly love might press on her.
Such sweetness touched her voice; the sacred quire

S. Cecilia.

Would hearken pleased, and voices not of earth
Mingled with hers harmonious, and she drew
From voice and hand such descants as the skies
Themselves had envied, as with pipe on pipe
Conjoined with wedded notes and varying tones
She made high music to our Lord in heaven.

Now, when this maiden lost in dreaming thought
Was of full age, her father bade her wed
A noble Roman youth, Valerian,
A Pagan yet ; but she, whose filial love
Constrained her to obey, beneath her robes
Of marriage hid a robe of penance still,
And to her husband, whom indeed she loved
With wifely love, confessed her mystic tale—
How night and day, whether she slept or woke,
A ghostly presence, standing at her side,
Kept watch and ward, nor left her. And when he
Asked sight of him, and proof, she bade him seek

The saintly Urban in the Catacombs,
Where he lay hid, and he consenting went,
And rose converted from his old unfaith
And was baptized; and when, a Christian now,
He sought his home again, he heard within
Enchanting music sweet, and strains divine;
And long time listening rapt, at last he came
To his wife's chamber, and beheld, indeed,
His eyes being opened by his faith, a form
Celestial standing by her, with a crown
Of roses in each hand, in scent and hue
Immortal, and the Angel as they knelt
Crowned each with them—the crown of martyrdom.

And then, because the Lord Valerian
Obeyed so well, the Angel bade him ask
What boon he would. And he: 'My lord, I have
A brother of my love, Tiburtius;
Let him believe.' And he made answer to him,

S. Cecilia.

'So shall it be, and ye shall both attain
The martyr's crown.'   And then he passed away.
And presently Tiburtius, entering,
Though yet he might not see the roses, knew
Their fresh immortal sweetness flood the air
With fragrance, and he heard the gracious words
Cecilia spake, and all her proofs inspired
Of Heaven and of the truth, and so his heart
Was touched and he baptized and held the Faith.

But when the Pagan Lord, Almachius,
Who governed, heard these things, he bade them cease
To call on Christ, and when they would not, sent them
To prison dungeons foul, and thence to death.

Last, when the brothers died, his pitiless rage
Summoned Cecilia.   Her, with threats of pain
And horrible death, he bade do sacrifice
To the false gods.   She, with a smile of scorn,

Denied him; and the people round who heard
Her constancy, wept for the fate they knew
Waited the fair girl-wife, and, bathed in tears,
Confessed themselves to be like her, of Christ,
Till the fierce prefect, mingling rage with fear,
Spake thus: 'What art thou, woman, who dost dare
Defy the gods?' And she, with lofty scorn:
'I am a Roman noble.' Then said he,
'I ask thee of thy faith?' And she: 'Oh, blind !
See these whom my example drew to Christ,
Take them for answer.'
     Then with panic haste
He sent a headsman whose keen axe should end
That high undaunted courage. He, with fear
And trembling hand, upon her slender throat
And virgin breast planting three cruel strokes,
Fled, leaving her for dead. But three days yet,
Three precious days, she lingered, strengthening all
Her converts in the Faith, and to the poor

S. Cecilia.

Vowing her wealth; and last of all she sent
For Urban, and besought him of his grace
That of her palace they should make a church
For Christian worship.
      Then she raised her voice
In soaring hymns of praise, and with her sang
The quire of Angels, chanting row on row
Celestial strains, and the rapt hearers knew
The sound of heavenly music and the lyres
Of the angelic company; and yet,
When her voice soared no longer, but was still,
Fair dying echoes, fainter and more faint,
Stole downward from the skies, and then were lost
Within the heavens—the music of a soul
Which joins the eternal concert and is blest.

And still where once she sang, the unfailing spell
Of music rises heavenward, day by day;
For, as she would, they built a stately church

Above her.   There, when centuries were past,
The Pontiff Paschal found her body lie,
Wrapt in a tissue of gold, and by her side
Her husband and his brother.

       And, again,
After long centuries they built a shrine,
And set in it a statue of the saint
In Parian marble.   On her side she rests
As one asleep; the delicate hands are crossed.
Wrist upon wrist; a clinging vestment drapes
The virgin limbs, and round her slender throat
A golden circlet masks her cruel wound.
And there she lies for all to see ; but still
Her voice is sounding in the Eternal Psalm
Which the Church singeth ever, evermore,
The Church on earth, the Church of Saints in Heaven."

SS. Adrian and Natalia.

And then it was a youthful pair who came,
And noble both, who to each other clung
In tender love: he a young soldier tall,
With the proud mien and port of one who strode
From the far North to the extremest South
Before Rome's conquering legions, o'er the world,
Bearing the eagles forth; she a fond wife,
Who clasped and kissed his hand, and gazed on him
With youthful eyes, while with the unbraided gold
Of her fair hair, bright as the crowns they wore,
He with pure yearning played. I knew them not,
Nor doth the world as yet, when thus my guide:

" Adrian, Tribune of the Imperial Guard,

When the tenth wave of blood assailed the Faith,
Served in Bithynia. There, a youth in years,
He lived in wedlock with his youthful love,
Natalia, fair, and virtuous as fair,
And secretly of Christ. When came command
That all should kneel before the heathen gods,
The brave S. George tore from the city walls
The shameful edict. Then, with coward rage,
The Pagan Cæsars in one day haled forth
Two score to death with torture. In the hall
Of judgment Adrian, as beseemed his rank,
Stood with his soldiers. Fierce and fiercer still
The torturers plied their hellish arts; and he,
Seeing how firm the martyrs stood and bore
Fell malice and the black despite of men,
Wondered to see their pious constancy.
Last, his great heart grew sickened at the wrong,
And then the strong resistless tide of Faith
Took him, and he believed, because he knew,

That this thing was of God; and his brave soul,
Which scorned concealment and the hypocrite's wiles,
Burst into word and act, and from his breast
He tore the glittering emblems of his rank,
And, flinging from him the dishonoured sword
Which served the Pagan, being now of Christ,
While all his soldiers wondered, knowing not
What thing he would, amid the painful throng
Of prisoners standing, cried aloud and said,
'I too am with them, for I am of Christ;
Torture me, slay me, too.' Then, with amaze,
The guards advancing haled him with the rest
To prison and to death. But he gave thanks
For what had been, and, glorying in his faith,
Went with his suffering brethren to his doom.

Now, when these things were done, there fell deep awe
And pity on all who heard, and to the house
Of Adrian hastened breathless messengers

To tell of what had been, and how its lord,
Spurning the Pagan gods, had braved his doom.
' Adrian is Christian and holds fast the Faith,
And goes to torture for his Master's name.'
Thus said they; and his wife, who heard the tale,
Felt her young heart beat slow, then cease with pain,
And swooned; but when her life returned again,
Gave thanks and wept for joy that he, her love,
Was worthy to bear witness to the Faith
And know a blessèd death.

                      Quickly she rose
And hastened to the prison cell, and there
Fell prone on his belovèd neck, and kissed
His heavy chains, giving God praise that he,
Like her, was of the Faith, and bade him keep
The Truth through death and torment to the end,
And comforted her love, and clasped him round,
And, on his dear lips showering kisses, went
Back to their lonely palace. Three long days

S.S. Adrian and Natalia.

She spent in prayer for him, on whom the fell
Forces of evil worked their will, and doomed
His life to cruel death; but never again,
Loving with all her tender heart, would dare
To seek his prison cell, lest haply Love
Should conquer Duty; but her faithful prayer
Rose for him day and night, that he might live
Or die, if such God's will, true to the Faith.

But on the prisoner, Adrian, longing came,
When now he was condemned and the new day
Should bring him death with pain, if only he
Might see his love once more, and when 'twas night,
Though firm and constant in the Faith and strong
To die for it, an innocent desire
To look once more in those belovèd eyes,
And press once more those stainless lips, and hear
Once more that tender voice, and seem again
A lover as of yore; and, offering gold

And giving surety for his safe return
Ere the dawn brought the day when he should die,
The prison doors flew open, and he stole—
Free once again, as if the fateful Past
Were but a dreadful nightmare of his sleep—
Forth from the dungeon's close and filthy air,
Through the cool night, by the familiar ways,
None in the darkness marking him, to where,
Within his palace halls, Natalia mused,
Sad, silent, lonely, half distraught in mind—
Sad she should see no more the well-loved face,
Glad that her love bare witness to the Faith—
Seeking to exorcise her painful thought
With spinning.   Then one hastened in and cried,
'Be of good heart, dear mistress, for my lord,
'Scaping the dungeon, comes and will be here.
Prepare for flight; you shall live happy yet.
Have all things ready.   Lo! the night is dark;

Take horse and flee.'

      Then through that faithful heart
A thousand warring tides of passion surged—
Hope, fear, love, duty, natural joy and pride
Because she was a wife and rapt in love;
But at the last, the passion of the Faith
Prevailing, prone to earth she fell, and cried,
'Ah, miserable me, who am too vile
To wed with one who wears the martyr's crown!
Shall not all men cry shame on me, whose love
Led Adrian astray, who else had dared
The fiercest torments which the devilish spite
Of Hell devised for him! Oh, my lost love,
'Twere better I should love thee thus, and bear
Part in thy glory, though it came with death,
Than live with thee dishonoured and, through me,
Sinking in coward fear the love of God.
Nay, my sweet Adrian, not for me indeed
Shalt thou deny the Faith.'

Now Adrian heard,
Standing without, his wife's belovèd voice,
And caught her words, and could not brook delay
An instant, but burst swiftly in and clasped her
Close to his heart, and lifting up his voice—
' Noblest and best of women, I give praise
To God that thou art strong, and that thy soul
Is steadfast as my own.   I do but come
To say to thee " Farewell," for with the day
I am condemned to die.   Full well I knew
Thy love would never tempt me to be false :
For only utter faithfulness is love.
But now thy loyal soul has smoothed my path
And left my duty easier, and I go
Back to my dungeon with a cheerful heart
That I have seen thy face.'
      Then she arose
And kissed him, and upon his breast she laid
Her wifely head ; and straight, without a word,

SS. Adrian and Natalia.

They twain went unattended through the night,
Who might have fled, and by the well-known streets,
Hushed now and slumbering; guarded by no guard
Save their own honour, sought the prison gate.
And, much amazed, the warder marked them come,
Hand clasped in hand, and swung the sounding door
And in his prison cell till dawn of day
They sate together, waiting for the end.

And Adrian, when the day was come, went forth
To judgment, and they scourged him sore and racked
His limbs with cruel tortures. But his wife
They drave forth from him, and he lay alone
On the cold ground, with none to comfort him,
Since well they knew what charity inspired
The womanly soft hearts which called on Christ;
And she, lamenting sore and half distraught
Because he suffered with no hand to soothe
His painful limbs, rose suddenly and took

A daring purpose. From her comely head
She sheared the golden treasure of her hair,
Donning man's garb, and gained the prison gate,
Disguised, nor known to any as she went,
A man with all a woman's pitying heart,
A woman with the courage of a man ;
And, gaining entrance, sought her love, and bound
His piteous wounds, soothed him with loving words.
' Light of mine eyes, how blest art thou,' she cried,
' To suffer for the Faith !' and strengthened him,
And lulled his pain to sleep, and with him sate,
Sleepless herself, his head upon her breast,
Filled with deep grief and saintly ecstasy,
Until the slow dawn, glimmering, brought the day.

Then, when the sun had risen, there came command
That he should die ; but first, with hateful art,
His good right hand they severed while he lived.
And she saw all, and watched without a word,

And all her tender woman's heart stood still
To see his pain, and fain had borne it all—
Filled with high pride, yet tortured with regret
That she had wrought this thing; and round him cast
Her wifely arms, prayed with him, and sustained
His ebbing life, till, ere the headsman came
To sever from the trunk the well-loved head,
With one deep sigh, he breathed his last and gave
His soul to God.

           But she, when all was done,
Kissed him upon the painless brow, and stooped
And took his severed hand, the dear dead hand
Which oft had smoothed her hair; and in her bosom,
Upon her wifely breast, she hid it close,
The dear dead hand! and, hurrying to her home,
Safe in her palace chamber folded it
With linen kerchiefs fine, and wrapt it round
With precious spices sweet and perfumed oils,
And by her lonely bedside kept it long,

And often, ere the grey dawn broke, would rise
And kiss and clasp it, giving thanks to God
That her love kept the Faith.
                        But the saint's body
Some faithful Christians stealing from the jail
Bore to Byzantium; there with pious care
They buried it, and costly obsequies.

But she, the sainted woman, dwelt alone
Long time within her palace, cherishing
The memory of her love. Cæsar at last,
Hating her constant soul, bade her prepare
For wedlock with some favourite of the Court,
A Tribune of the Guard. No word she breathed
Of disobedience, but one night she fled
Her widowed home, and, taking ship, sailed forth
To Argyropolis, across the sea;
And when they told her how her love was laid
Hard by, within a costly sepulchre,

Dwelt there long time, grown happier that she held
Her love's belovèd dust.   Oft in the night
She rose and took her to the tomb, and there
Knelt, and full often in her weary sleep,
Heavy with tears, the blessed Adrian
Visited her in dreams, and shone on her
Bright with the glory of beatitude,
Beckoning that she should follow, till her soul,
Straining its earthly fetters, longed to rise
And join her love in bliss.   And so at length
Her fervent prayer was granted.   Death set free
That faithful heart; and when at last, it loosed
Her prisoned spirit, lo! a glorious quire
Of Angels, and amid them Adrian,
To meet her as she rose; and sphere on sphere
They soared together heavenward into joy,
Where are the just of old, the seers, the saints
And witnesses, and there, no more to part,
Bathed in the full light of the Heavenly Sun,

They dwell together for ever and are blest."

And as I listened, rapt in tearful thought,
And musing on the mystery of Pain
That wings the saintly soul, I heard again:

"Not only through the dungeon or the rack
Is won the Martyr's crown.   Blest souls indeed
Are those which suffer openly, and reap
Through bodily pain the rich reward of Love—
Dear souls and strong; but those who only bear
The suffering of the soul, when the racked spirit
Gives love for faith, and dooms a life to die,
Dearer than life, for duty, and lives on
And bears and does not die, but wears its pain
For weary years, and hears no loud acclaim
Of heavenly quires, and bears no victor's palm,
But lives self-doomed to solitude and doubt,

And finds the closed heavens deaf, the past a dream,
And all the future dumb—for these, too, Heaven
Keeps its own crown, as precious as the pearl
Of sacrifice which decks the painful brow
Of agony,—its own triumphant crown.
For what is martyrdom but witness borne
To God and Truth, in body as in soul,
Through life and death, though sudden stress of pain
Or life-long suffering witness to the Right?"

'Twas an old man came next, who bore the palm,
Mild and of venerable mien, with hair
And beard of silver, yet his sunburnt cheek
Showed ruddy with the hue of health which still
Smiles like an Indian summer on the lives
Of those who, like the first great Husbandman,
Breathe purer air far from the dust of towns,
And watch the fair flowers blow, the fruits grow ripe,
Changing their healthy toil for tranquil sleep,
And mingling works of mercy with pure thoughts
And meditations. Him indeed I knew not,
And yet half guessed his tale.
      And this it was:

S. Phocas.

"In Pontus, by Sinope, dwelt of old,
Three centuries after Christ, an agèd man,
Phocas by name. He to his lowly home
Retiring from the busy city, spent
His life in meditation on the Faith,
Sweetening his honest toil. Day after day
Within his narrow garden-ground he found
Fit labour for his hands; eve after eve,
When the sweet toilsome day at last was done,
He strayed among the flowers and fruits his skill
Had reared—the roses red and white which filled
The air with perfume, like the fragrant flower
Of sanctitude; the white cups veined with gold
Of lilies, pure as blameless lives, which breathe
Their sweetness to the heavens; the flower which bears
The symbols of the Passion; the mild roots
And milky herbs which nourish those white lives
That scorn to batten on the blood and pain

Of innocent dumb brutes; such honeyed fruits
As our first parents ate in Paradise—
Rich apples, golden pears, pink pomegranates,
The pendent purple of the trellised grape,
And blushing peaches, and the perfumed globes
Of melons; all the flowers and fruits the isles
Of the enchanted dim Hesperides
Bore in the fabled eld. Of these he took
Sufficient for his hunger, praising God,
And of the rest he gave of charity
To all the poor and weak, free without price,
Following his Master's word. And all the poor
And needy blessed him and revered the skill
Which reared them, and the venerable years
Of that good gardener. None who came to him
His generous hand denied, but he would give them
Shelter and food, and, when the day was done,
Converse on things Divine, and many a word
Of Truth which swayed the listener, if he were

A Pagan still, or heartened him indeed
If he already held and loved the Faith.

For while to some pure souls the thought, the dream,
The blessèd vision are enough, the sounds
Heard by rapt ears, the opened heavens, the joy
Of contemplation only, when the sands
Of the desert or the cloistered vistas dim
Show ghostly 'neath the midnight stars, for some
Labour is best—not sordid labour vile
And turned to earth, but that which working still
For Heaven doth therefore gain a purer height
Than any; and for him the varied page
Of Nature painted by a hand divine
Brought meditation, and he found a voice
In every bursting flower and mellowing fruit;
In every life which, governing its way,
By heavenly rule, lived on without offence
And did fulfil its part; in every weed

Which cumbered earth, yet doubtless were of aid
If we might read its secret; every growth
Of poison, which from the same elements,
The bounteous earth, the wooing of the sun,
The same fair fanning breezes, as the grain
On which our lives are nourished, waxed and grew
To deal out death and torment.   Long he mused
On all these things—how one great Husbandman
Planted them all, and framed them as He framed
The tiger and the lamb; and so he gained
Mild wisdom from his daily task, and awe,
And wonder, which is kin to faith, and thence
True faith in God and man, and was content
To sow the seed of good within his soul,
As in the earth, and root the evil out,
And living only for the Faith, to work
And be at peace, leaving the rest to Him
Who sends in season, sun and rain and cloud
And frost, and in whose hand are flower and fruit

S. Phocas.

To give or to withhold, in earth and heaven.

Now, one fair summer eve, as Phocas sate
At supper, came a knock, and he in haste
Opening, three strangers waited at the door,
Whom he bade enter and take food and rest;
And when they were refreshed, he questioned them
What errand brought them. And they said in turn,
'We seek a certain Phocas—know'st thou him?—
Who dares to call on Christ, and have command
To slay him found.' Then tranquilly the saint—
'Sleep now and rest. I know him. With the dawn
I will conduct you to him.' And they slept,
Not dreaming whom they saw, and were content.

But he, when all the house was dark and still,
Stole out into his garden. The faint stars,
Pale in the radiance of the summer night,
Trembled above him; at his feet the flowers

He loved so well declined their heavy heads
And slumbering petals.   One loud nightingale,
Thrilling the tender passionate note of old,
Throbbed from a flower-cupped tree, and round him all
The thousand perfumes of the summer night
Steeped every sense in fragrance sweeter far
Than frankincense the skill of men compounds
In Araby the Blest.   Then on the grass
He sate him down, rapt deep in musing thought;
And o'er him, ghostly white or gleaming red,
The roses glimmered, and the lilies closed
Their pure white cups, and bowed their heads, and seemed
To overhear his thought.   'Should he then fly,
To live a little while, leaving his home
And all that made it dear, the flowers, the fruits
He loved, and preach the Faith a little yet
Before Fate called him?   Surely life is sweet
To tranquil souls, which scorn delights and take
Something of Heaven on earth; ay, sweeter far

Than the old haste of flushed and breathless chase,
Strong pulses, vaulting projects, hot designs
To capture worthless ends.   Haply 'twere well
For this, to leave the solitude he loved
As others wife or child.'
                      But as he mused,
The thought of full obedience filled his soul;
Submissive to the Heavenly Will which sent
Those fatal messengers, and destined for him
The martyr's crown, and swayed and took so fast
His doubtful mind, that presently he rose,
As one whose purpose halts not—rose and went
As in a dream, and coming brought a spade
And softly, half in dreams, began to delve
The flower-lit turf, within a sheltered nook
O'ergrown with roses and the perfumed gloom
Of blossomed trees.   And as he wrought, he laid
Turf upon turf, and hollowed out a space
In the fresh virgin mould which lay beneath,

Shaped deftly in the semblance of a cross,
Large as might take the stature of a man.
And still half dreaming, nor confessing yet
What thing he did, deeper and yet more deep
He dug and laboured, till with earliest dawn,
Just as the waking birds began their song,
He flung the last mould upwards, smoothing fair
The edges of the trench, and knew at length
That all night long he laboured at his grave.

And at its foot were lilies white and gold,
And at its head were roses white and red,
And all around a pitying quire of flowers
Bent down regarding it ; and when he saw,
Still half as in a dream, he whispered, 'Lo !
The narrow bed is ready ; ere 'tis day
The sleeper shall be laid in it, and prove]
Unbroken slumbers blest, until the peal
Of the loud Angel wakes him from the skies.'

S. Phocas.

Then to his home returning grave and slow,
He sought his guests, on whom the new-born day
Was rising. They with half-awakened eyes
Greeted their coming host, and, bidding him
Good morrow, rose and took the frugal meal
His care provided. Then the question came,
'Hast brought him whom we seek?' And he: 'I have.'
And they: 'Where find we him?' And he: 'Behold,
I am the man—none else.' Then deep distress
Took them, and great perplexity, who knew
The man whose life they sought the same who gave
Shelter and food. But he, revolving all,
The martyr's palm and that unchanged resolve
Of the still night, bade them take heart for all
Their duty bade them. And he led them forth,
Through maiden flowers fresh opened to the day,
Brushing the dewdrops from them as they went
To where, set round with blooms, they found his grave

Fresh delved in daisied turf, and there they bound
Their willing prisoner, and the headsman's axe,
Even as he knelt, a smile upon his lips,
By one swift, skilful blow and merciful,
Upon the grassy margin, painlessly
Severed his life. And there they laid him down,
Amid the joyous matins of the birds,
In the sweet earth ; and by his head there sprang
Lush roses red and white, and by his feet
Deep chaliced lilies mingled white with gold ;
And there he waits the day the just shall rise
And bloom, as these on earth, beyond the skies."

But when I heard the gracious tale, which showed
Like some fair blossom with a fragrant heart,
Thus would I answer : " Blameless anchorite,
Meek martyr, self-betrayed, some saints there be
Whose youthful suffering draws a readier tear

Than thine; and yet, for me, that duteous life
Of honest toil for others, that great faith
Thou show'dst, that simple eagerness to bear
The martyr's palm, that night beneath the stars
Of summer, fashioning thy flower-decked grave,
That lonely suffering, mark thy life and death
With a more calm and gracious note than theirs
Who, 'mid the applauding saints around, the throng
Of heavenly faces stooping from the skies,
In the arena dauntless met their end;
A simpler nor less touching piety
Than theirs who, 'mid the dust of mortal strife,
Shed their pure lives upon the sullen sand."

And then there passed a beautiful fair maid,
A virgin martyr, from whose comely head
Shone brighter than her crown, a ray serene
Of stainless purity. Her spotless robe
Gleamed with strange light, and at her breast she bore
Celestial lilies and a fragrant spoil
Of roses red and white, red as the blood
Of Martyrdom, white as the innocent life
Of maidenhood; and straight I knew the name
Of Dorothea, whose fair story fires
Poet and painter still; and as I gazed
I heard, with eager ears, my guide recount
The half-remembered tale, and thus he spake:

S. Dorothea.

"In Cæsarea dwelt a noble maid,
A Christian, serving God with prayer and alms
And fasting.   None more beautiful or pure
In all the city, and her fitting name
Was Dorothea.   And the fame of her,
Her beauty, and her saintly life went forth
Through all the country.
                       When the governor,
Who hated Christ, holding the older creed,
Heard of her name and deeds, he gave command
That they should bring her to him.   On a day
He sate on high in judgment, when they brought
The maid; and she, with mantle folded close
Around her, and chaste downcast eyes, drew near,
When he with threatening voice would ask of her,
'Who art thou?'   And the maiden: 'Sir, my name
Is Dorothea, and I serve the Lord.'
Then he, with fury: 'Thou shalt serve our gods

Or die the death.'   But she, with accents mild :
' If I shall die, the sooner shall my eyes
Behold His Presence whom they long to see.'
And he : ' Whom namest thou ?'   Then she : ' The
　　　Lord,
In whom I live, who is my Heavenly Spouse,
Who dwells in Paradise, with whom I long
To be, leaving this dead poor earth, and know
The heavenly fruits that in His garden ripe,
The roses that shall never fade, but bear
Such amaranthine blooms as heat nor cold
Withers, nor time, but blush for ever sweet.
Work thou thy will.   For me to die is gain,
And to live, loss ; but for thy Pagan gods,
I will have none of them, nor sacrifice
To wood or stone, the figments of men's hands.'

Then he, who could not bend that steadfast soul,
Commanded they should take her to her cell.

S. Dorothea.

Thither he summoned an apostate pair,
Christita and Calista, once of Christ,
On whom the fear of swift and painful death,
The terror of the torments which the spite
Of men prepared for them, worked in such sort
That they renounced the Faith and knelt again
Before the old false gods. To these he gave
Great promise of reward if they should make
This noble virgin partner in their sin,
And to her prison cell, day after day,
Despatched them, and they strove to do his will,
Using the coward's weapons,—fear of death,
Hope of some baser happiness, and doubts
If 'twere indeed of God the Faith she held,
Or if 'twere haply best to live and serve
The elder gods to whom their fathers knelt;
And how 'twas sweeter far to know the love
Of spouse and children, and the joys of home,
Than to fling life away upon a dream,

And feel the ravening tigers' jaws, the bite
Of the keen flames, withering the flesh, the keen
Thin knives, the crushing rack, and all the arts
Of the tormentors' hands.   But as they spake
She with such faith reproved their perfidy
That in despair they ceased.

       At last, in turn,
With such clear thought and Heaven-sent utterance
She bore on them; dressed with such precious robes
The beauty of the Truth; spurned with such power
The Pagan lie; showed with such pitying love
The misery of unfaith, the joys they lost
Who did deny the Faith, knowing it true
And having once believed; that suddenly,
As self-convicted by the accusing voice
Of their own selves, those weak apostate souls
Shrank from her as from a consuming fire,
And, grown repentant of their wrong, confessed
Their fault, and, falling down before her feet,

Besought her she would pray for them, and seek
Remission of their sins ; and she, indeed,
With great joy kneeling with them, sought in prayer
Forgiveness for their fault, and when they rose,
She kissed them, and they went, with steadfast voice
And joyful, openly confessing Christ.

But when the tyrant learnt what thing had been,
He gave command that those poor penitents
Should die by fire before the virgin's eyes,
That she might share their pain. The fierce flames leapt,
The hapless sisters suffered, giving praise.
And Dorothea watched their pangs, and cried,
' Fear not, dear sisters ; suffer to the end,
And take for price of those brief fleeting pains
Eternal bliss in Heaven.' So they died firm.
And she, in turn before the tyrant brought,
Was doomed to instant death. But ere she died
They racked her tender limbs, while she gave thanks

And bore their worst unmoved; and then they led her
To where the headsman with his gleaming axe
Awaited her, and with him welcome Death.

But as she passed, there rose the mocking voice
Of one, a lawyer, who, when first the maid
Was brought to judgment, mocked the words she spake
Of the sweet flowers and fruits of Paradise,
Which ever in the garden of the Lord
Spring in perpetual beauty; nor doth there
Snow come, nor frost, but evermore the heavens
Smile on them, and they ripen, and they breathe
Celestial odours fine, celestial hues
Brighten them, and whoso shall take of them
Shall taste eternal bliss. Seeing her pass,
And mindful of her words, inflamed with scorn,
His shallow witless mirth and Pagan spite
Broke forth. 'Fair maiden hastening to thy Spouse,
Send me, I pray thee, of the fruits, the flowers

Of His celestial garden; for with us
'Tis winter, and no flowers nor fruits are here,
But only clouds and snows and bitter winds,
Scourging the naked fields.   Send me of them,
For fain am I to take them.'   As he spake
The maiden, bending, with a gentle smile,
Answered, ' I will.'   And he, with scoffs and jeers,
Turned with his graceless fellows, mocking her;
But she went calm and cheerful to her death.

Now, when she reached the place where she should die,
She knelt awhile, bowing her head in prayer;
And when she rose prepared for death, there came
A precious portent.   For beside her stood,
To comfort her, a youthful Angel fair,
With locks of gold, and eyes as blue as Heaven:
And in his hands he bore, so runs the tale,
A basket, and, within, three golden fruits
Of Paradise, of scent and hue divine,

And with them three fair roses, sweeter far
Than the twice-bearing Pæstine gardens bare,
Summer and autumn.   Then, with a sweet smile
Of Faith triumphant : ' Pray you, good my lord,
Carry these fruits and flowers to him who spake
While I was passing to my death, and say,
" 'Tis Dorothea sends them, and she goes
Before thee to the garden whence they came,
And doth await thee there." '

        Then with the word
She bent her gentle neck upon the block,
And took the blow which sped her soul to Heaven.

Now, as she died, the scoffing lawyer stood
Among his comrades, jesting at the gift
The maiden promised.   But when now they sate
Feasting, around them gilded images
Of the false gods, taking no care nor thought
For what had been, the torture and the pain,

S. Dorothea.

Lo! suddenly a heavenly presence showed,
From whence he knew not, fair, with shining face,
And locks of gold, and eyes as blue as Heaven,
And in his hand a basket with the fruits
And flowers of Paradise, who spake no word
But, 'Dorothea sends them, and she goes
Before thee to the garden whence they came,
And doth await thee there,' and having said,
Vanished as he had come.
      And the youth's heart
Was touched with awe and pity, and he rose,
And his heart melted, and he seemed to take
Of the celestial fruit, as one who takes
The Eucharistic bread; and straight his soul
Rose to new life, and held the Faith, and owned
The Holy Name, and bore like her his pain,
And passed from pain to life, and gained the crown
Of martyrdom, and is like her in joy."

And when he ceased, my soul within me cried,
" Oh, sweet celestial flowers and fruits divine,
Which are good words and faithful deeds that spring
From flower to fruit in Heaven ! Shall any hear
This precious legend with a heart unmoved
By the ineffable gifts whose sign ye are—
The flower of loving words, which can disarm
The brute within our hearts ; the precious fruit
Of faithful deeds, which he who tastes and makes
His own shall find indeed a heavenly food—
Strengthen his strength, make clean his soul, and breed
New thoughts within him, till his lower self,
Sunk deep in sense, dull, gross, denying Heaven,
Falls down from him, and, a new creature, comes
To soar through suffering to a higher life."

And then there seemed a breach in the long ranks
Of saintly lives.   Till then I heard the tale
Of martyrdoms where the fierce Pagan raged
Against the nascent faith.   Henceforth my dream
Was chiefly of white lives, which gained the crown
By too great scorn of self, who gave to Heaven
Not of its own alone, but part of earth's,
And yet grew blessèd.   Martyrdoms there were,
Even as of old, when with fierce bigot rage
Christian with Christian striving, plied anew
The Pagan's hellish arts of pain and death,
The dungeon and the stake, the rack, the sword,
Seeking—oh, shameful thought !—to chase from earth
The heretic God bore with.   None of these

I saw, or seeing, asked not of my guide,
Because my soul grew sick, and could not bear
The piteous tale. But of self-sacrifice—
Lavish, indeed, yet blest—high sacrifice
Vowed to great ends and blest, my ears were full,
As one in pilgrim's garb, ascetic, seared,
Still with some ghost of pain, and some faint trace
Of sadness in his eyes, and yet withal,
Despite his humble garb and lowly port,
A Roman noble, met my curious gaze ;
And this the tale I heard :

"When the first Innocent was Pope of Rome,
A Senator there was, Euphemian,
Who long with Aglaë, his wife, had prayed,
Having great riches and no heir to take them,
For offspring of their love. At length their prayer
Was granted, and a son was born to them,
Alexis, fair of body and white of soul.

Him the pure vision through his growing years
Failed not, but always on his life there shone
The light of the Unseen, so that he fared
Through all the heats of youth a soul unstained,
Clothed in the spotless garb of innocence,
And, 'mid the pomps of rank and riches, still
Lived evermore in great humility
As lived his Master, and still kept a heart
Touched with compassion for the poor and weak;
And, being purer than the rest, was fain,
Through self-contempt and saintly diffidence,
To mortify the sinful flesh, and make
A daily penance for the wrong he loathed.

Therefore, while outwardly in silk and gold,
The emblems of his proud patrician birth,
He showed before men's eyes, he bore beneath,
Seeking to mortify this load of flesh,
Next to his flesh, a painful vest of hair;

And, though he walked before men's eyes a bright
And smiling presence, in his secret cell
Bewailed with vigils and with tears the wrong
He never did, a pure soul bowed and bent
By the great burden of the sinful world.

Thus sped the fleeting years, which crowned his youth
With manhood. Never did his dreaming thought
Turn to the earth or earthly things, but still
The heavens stood open ; the immortal youth
Of the adoring angels dimmed the charm
Of earthly beauty, and he lived apart,
Like that rapt boy who saw as in a glass
A fair reflected image in the stream,
And loved it only. Then the sire and dame,
Because they fain would see their noble tree
Blossom before they died, would urge their son
That he should wed, and named to him a maid
Fair, modest, high of birth, higher of soul,

Whom from a child he knew, and well had loved;
And he, long time delaying, at the last,
Being dutiful and fain to do their will,
Consented, and the glad day dawned when they
Together in God's house, bridegroom and bride,
Knelt at the altar, and the vows were pledged
And the words spoken which should make them one.

So all day long the joyous marriage feast
Sped gaily to the cheerful sound of song.
But from his bride, her soft eyes looking love,
The young Alexis stood apart, and mused
As one whom some deep sorrow presses down;
And through the long halls passing, sad, distraught,
To all the greetings of the courtly throng
Made hardly answer. For before his eyes
Ever the beatific dream of old,
The virginal whiteness of the saints, the pure
Angelic faces bent before the throne,

Filled all his musing thought, until the feast,
The acclaiming friends, the mirth, nay, the meek face
Of his young bride, showed dim and scarcely seen
Before his rapturous gaze; nor could he brook
The innocent thoughts of love fulfilled which flush
The dreams of youth.   Such thoughts were not for one
Who had seen the opened heavens, the throng of saints,
And the pure Virgin Mother; not for him
The pulse of earthly passion.   Could he dare
To quench in deeps of sense the pale white fire
Of the ascetic soul?   Could mortal love
Allure him from his heavenly home, or turn
His duteous thought to earth?   Nay, nay; he could not.
A stern voice bade him fly, while yet 'twas time.
And yet 'twas hard to leave the home he loved
And those who loved him.   But what said the Word?
' Who leaves not father, mother, wife, and child
For Me and for My kingdom, loves not me.'
' Love I not thee, oh Lord?   Shall not I dare

S. Alexis.

To give all things for Thee? And yet Thy Word
Bids each man, leaving all, cleave to his wife.
How shall I dare desert her in her grief?
How shall I bear to leave her to men's spite
And mockery—a wife her husband shuns,
A bride yet not a wife. And my dear sire,
And gracious mother? Is not wedlock blest,
And are they not of Thee? Do I not cast
Reproach on those white souls, who lived in pure
And blessed union? If our Lord on earth
Dwelt in His father's house, and deigned to be
In Cana, at the marriage feast, nor scorned
To make the water wine, why should not I—
Being but a worm, indeed, a thing of nought,
Too low, too vile for Heaven, too weak for earth—
Why should not I, taking my humble part
In the great throng of life, foregoing all
My dim celestial dream, bearing the cross
In all humility, accept my part,

Rearing my children in the fear of God
And love of Christ, hastening the blessèd hour
When all the world is His, and He shall tread
All earthly crowns beneath His feet and reign
A King among His saints? Surely 'twere best
To advance His kingdom thus?' And then he turned
Back to the joyful feast, and sate beside
His innocent love, regarding well content
Her fair unsullied beauty, and would strive
To take the joyous greetings of his kin,
And look with loving glances on his bride.

So all day long the joyous marriage feast
Sped gaily to the cheerful noise of song.
And now the sun had sunk beyond the west,
And night had fallen, when a dread voice seemed
To summon him away, bidding him fly
The world and worldly joys. So clear it came
And awful to his ear, he could not stay,

S. Alexis.

He durst not tarry. 'I have need of thee,
Alexis'—so it spake. And he, who heard
The voice as of the Lord, without a doubt,
Obedient to the heavenly summons, rose
And sought his bride; and on her hand he set,
In token of his love and troth, a ring
Of purest gold, and round her slender waist
A zone of precious gems, and on her head
A veil of costly purple. Then in tears,
The dread voice calling always, with one kiss
He left her, and flung forth into the night,
Unseen, and no man found him till he died.

Then through that hapless house there went a sound
Of wailing. All the ways they searched to find
The truant, but in vain; and straight their joy
Was turned to grief, and they in garb of woe
Sate mourning, without hope, the son, the spouse,
Whom never should they see until the end.

But when the bridegroom fled into the night,
Leaving behind him light and life and love,
Obedient always to the heavenly voice
Which summoned him away, his faltering steps
Led him to Tiber's bank, whereon he found
A little boat ; and, clad in pilgrim's garb,
All night he laboured seaward, till he came
To Ostia. There a bark in act to sail
For Asia took him, and he crossed the deep,
An exile self-pursued. No vain regret
For vanished riches held him, or lost love,
Or for the toil and hunger which he knew,
Following the heavenly voice, and so content.
Only at times some shade of doubt would come,
Considering all his mother's love, his sire
Left childless, and the sad surprise which filled
His bride's sweet eyes when he would go from her,
And how the house stood empty of delight,

And how those innocent lives must pine and droop
That he might do God's will; and all the load
And tangle of the too-perplexèd world !

So, after storm-tost days, he gained at length
The Syrian shore, and there long time he lived,
A hermit, at Edessa, lone, unknown,
Spending his days in alms, his nights in prayer,
Till gradually through the land his fame
Waxed, and the people's voice acclaimed him saint.
Then he, who wept his vileness and was filled
With saintly thoughts of deep humility,
Fled once again, sailing across the sea
For Tarsus, where of old the sainted Paul
Hallowed the earth.
    But a great tempest rose,
And drove the ship for many a darkling day
Far from her course; and when the sky grew clear,
Behold, the well-remembered coast again

By Ostia, where the yellow Tiber stains
The purple depths of the Tyrrhenian Sea,
And, lost in distance on the northern sky,
Rome and the stately palace of his sires.

But when Alexis saw the well-known shore
Hard by his ancient home, straightway his soul
Was filled once more with doubt, because he knew
That 'twas the Lord who ruled the storm, and drave
The strong ship from her course ; and when he mused
On all the past, how the strange people turned
His humbleness to pride, it seemed indeed
That here was his best sacrifice—to live
Within his father's house, unseen, unknown.
For since long years of penury had worked
Their will on him, and seared his cheek, and bent
His body, and bleached his hair, and hardly left
The embers of his youth, he might deceive
The gaze of loving eyes.

S. Alexis.

            So he set forth,
Wrapped in his pilgrim's cloak, along the still
Dead marsh, a solitary wayfarer,
Slow, leaning on his staff, obscured with dust
And weariness, until, at last, with eve
Rome and the stately palace of his sires.

Now when he gained the lofty gate where dwelt
His noble sire, the loved home of his youth
And manhood, where his fair unwedded wife
Still pined for him, the Lord Euphemian
Went forth with all his pomp; and as he passed,
Alexis—knowing all the work of time
And toil and fastings, and his whitened hair,
His furrowed brow, his straight form bowed and bent,
His ragged garb, which was a robe of silk,
And all the change, whose briefer name is age—
Stood forth, and threw him at his feet, and sought
Some humble food and shelter. And his sire,

Knowing his son was meek and pitiful
Of all the poor and weak, and how, perchance,
He, too, was now a wanderer poor as this,
Was touched with ruth and raised the suppliant,
Bade him be of good cheer, and signed to them
Who followed, they should give him food and place
Beneath his palace roof, and, charging them
That he should want for nothing, went his way;
Nor knew he by his blood's unwonted thrill
That 'twas his son he looked on. So once more
Within his father's house Alexis lay.

But those his careless menials, knowing naught
Of what had been, and deeming him no more
Than the poor wayworn wanderer he seemed,
Beneath the marble staircase of the house,
Found him some darkling cell, wherein he stayed
Being gentle and of great humility;
And seeing him so meek, no chiding word

E'er passed his uncomplaining lips, they deemed,
With the dull insolence of servitude,
That 'twas some idiot, weak of speech and brain,
Who lay there; and they plucked his beard and smote
His patient cheek, and on his suffering head
Heaped dust and ashes. But he spake no word
Reproachful of them, knowing well indeed
How great the load of his offence, and how
The Lord of all was mocked upon the Tree.
So in the house where he was heir to all,
He lay long years, knowing the bitter bread
Of penury, and cold, and all despite.
Long years he lived, below the lowest slave
In food and lodging, who was heir to all.

But harder than all else it was to bear
The daily, nightly sights and sounds of home;
To see his mother, ageing day by day,
Pass forth, still mourning for her son, and fear

To meet the eyes which, had they met his own,
Piercing his secret through, had ended all;
To know himself the cause of grief and woe
To her who bore him; yet withhold the word
Which spoken had brought joy to innocent hearts!

And most of all things was it grief to him,
In the dead hours when all beside was still,
Nightly to hear the sound of grief and tears,
And know the voice of her who was his bride,
Widow ere wedded. 'Whither, love, art gone?'
So wailed the voice; 'and wherefore didst thou wed,
To leave me thus to mourn for thee, and bear
Despite and scorn of men? Are we not one,
Knit by the law of God,—one flesh, one soul,
One being, fused by the mysterious word
Which spoken joined our lives? Return! return!
I weary for thy voice. Return! oh love!
But thou art far across the pitiless seas,

Or, haply, 'mid the sunless ways of death!'

Night after night the wailings came and pierced
His heart, and banished sleep, and wrung his soul
With torture; for the suffering of the soul,
Deeper than bodily anguish piercing, wears
The writhing life. For sometimes he would dream
He heard the voice, and then a mocking fiend
Would chide him for his flight, and whisper, ' Rise.
Duty lies plain before thee. Rise and seek
Thy injured wife; ask pardon of thy sire,
And her thy mother. Pride it was—nought else—
Apeing contrition, drove thee, that thou wert
Not as the world, the dim unnoted throng
Of those for whom the trivial daily road
Lies between lilies. Rise and take thy place,
Bearing the wholesome load of common life,
As did thy sires before thee.'
      Then the saint:

'I may not know if I do right indeed,
Such doubt o'erclouds my soul; but this I know—
There is a whiteness in virginity;
There is a virtue in the life withdrawn
By desert sands or antred wilds, apart
From wealth, and ease, and crowded haunts of men.
There, on the vigils of the saints, the skies
Burst open sudden, and the Mother of God
Opens her virgin arms and clasps her Son,
Virgin like her; and round the throne there shine
Angels and high archangels, row on row,
Pure all and virgin; and below them stand
The virgin martyrs. These my eyes have seen;
These, when the desert stars shone clear and cold,
And lions roared around the springs; these, too,
These, when the hot noon quivered round the palms,
The opening heavens revealed. And shall I bear
To tread the flowery paths of life and sink
To earthly joys? Nay, I am vowed, I am vowed!

S. Alexis.

The fields grow white, the harvest of the Lord
Ripens, and shall men dream of wedlock, now
At the full end and judgment of the world?'

Then with divided soul Alexis rose—
It was the dead of night—and through the long
Hushed corridors, with noiseless footfall, sought,
If haply he might see his love again,
Himself unseen, the well-remembered door;
And, pausing at the threshold, spied within
His maiden consort, kneeling bathed in tears,
Keeping a vigil for the man she mourned,
And heard her loving lips pronounce his name
In grief. 'Alexis, whither art thou gone?
Return, my love, return!'
       Even where he stood,
Hid by the arras, reached the wailing voice,
And, by her lamp's dim light, he saw the lines
On the belovèd brow, which time and grief

Had drawn, and all for him; and then great ruth
And yearning took him, and he longed to speak.
But while he mused, loud on his watching ear
A voice, which seemed of God, arose and hushed
All thoughts beside. 'Alexis, be thou strong.'

Then, with a groan as of a breaking heart,
His grief burst into utterance, and sighed,
'No more, dear wife, no more!'
                                  And then he stole,
Ghost-like, to his own place.
                            But she who heard
The words, and knew the voice, gazed with wide eyes.
Then swooned, as 'twere his spirit greeting her;
Nor slept, but with the morning told the tale,
And, grieving deep, was somewhat comforted
To think that he had come to her from Heaven.

And he, when he had gained his poor retreat,

S. Alexis.

Slept not.   His suffering heart was riven in twain,
His limbs refused their office, and his voice
Grew feeble, as by sickness marred, or age.
Nor from his humble pallet ever again
Rose he, but sank, with every day that came,
To deeper weakness still.   At last he knew
His hour was come, and so implored of one
Who tended him, the means to write; and then
A letter wrote he, setting forth at large
The truth of all these things, and his sad life,
And prayed forgiveness of his sins, and hid
The scroll within his vesture, next his heart;
And then his face grew calmer, and his eye
As of a saint in glory.   Till one day
They found him in his poor cell, lying dead,
Clasping the letter, on his face a smile.

Now, when Alexis lay in act to die,
It chanced that very day Pope Innocent

Said solemn Mass for Cæsar, and the Court
Knelt round, and, with the rest, Euphemian.
And when the mystic sacrifice was done,
And the proud concourse turned in act to go,
From the high altar pealed a voice which said
In solemn accents, 'Seek the holy man
Who this day comes to die, and ask of him
His prayers for Rome;' and while in awe they stayed
Expectant, then the strange voice once again—
'Go, seek him of the Lord Euphemian.'
And he, who heard it, knew not what the words
Meant, but, the Emperor bidding him, went forth
To gain his home, while after him there came
Cæsar and all the Fathers of the Church,
With long-drawn pomp, the Pontiff at their head.

Now, when Euphemian gained his stately house,
Lo! dark upon the gleaming marble stair
The slaves had laid a lifeless body down

To carry forth for burial ; and they said
To him who questioned them, ' My gracious Lord,
This was the pilgrim whom thou bad'st us take
Beneath thy roof years since, and he till now
Hath dwelt here of thine alms. An hour ago
He died, and soon we bear him to his grave ;
But in his grasp he holds a secret scroll
Which never would he part with, night or day.
See ! will it please you look upon his face ? '

Then, with great awe, the Lord Euphemian
Drew near the bier, remembering the voice
Which sent him there and bade him kneel and ask
A blessing of the dead, like him of old
Who fed the holy angels unawares,
And, marked with reverent eyes the pilgrim garb,
The scroll grasped tight within the wasted hand,
And all the marks of saintly poverty,
Nor knew on whom he looked. But when he drew

The face-cloth from the visage of the dead,
His life stood still; for straight the father's heart,
Through all disguise of penury and years,
Leapt to his son. For, lo! the wayworn face
Grew young in death, a smile was on the lip
As of old time, but round the saintly head
There shone a glory brighter than the day—
Sign of his rank in Heaven; and on his knees
The father fell before the son, and wept,
Giving God praise. And while he knelt, there came
Cæsar and Pontiff, and they knelt with him;
And the Pope reverently pressed the hand
Stiffened in death, beseeching of the dead
That he should give the scroll. And straight his grasp,
Relaxing, yielded; and the Chancellor
Read to the assembled nobles the strange tale
Of Life and Death, which thou hast heard to-day.

But when within the house the news was told,

The childless mother and the widowed wife,
Descending, threw themselves upon the bier,
Kissing the wasted form; plunged deep in woe,
Yet taking comfort that the dead they loved
Reigned now among the saints. Seven days and nights
They watched and wept before him, and a throng
Of halt and sick, and many a one was healed
Of his infirmity. Such things the saint
Wrought, with God's help, upon them for their faith.

Then, lest some secular use might mar the place
Made sacred by his pain, upon the ground
Where stood that stately house, they reared the Church
Of S. Alexis, and the marble stair
Which sheltered him they left as when he died.
And there a sculptor carved him, in mean garb
Reclining, by his side his pilgrim's staff,
And in his hand the story of his life
Of virgin pureness and humility."

And, when the tale was done, again my guide:
"Shall any scoff, deeming the sacrifice
Was vain, a sheer self-torment all unasked,
Which wrecked four innocent lives? Does God then ask
Such service of His creatures? Does He cast
Contempt upon His gracious paths of life,
Which all alike may tread—the precious flowers
Which, by the sacred light and warmth of home,
Bloom fragrant to the skies; the childish eyes
Which bring back Heaven; the priceless liturgies
Of daily fruitful sacrifice; the joys
Shared, and so doubled; all the blessèd pain
Of loss; the open grave; the sacred grief
That lifts us from the earth? Nay, nay, our lives
Are double, and our souls, as fitting those
Who move from earth to Heaven. Life has its joys,
And all may take them blameless. Yet there is
A something higher, too, than these—a thrill
Of ecstasy, a perfect path which hangs
Heavenward upon the everlasting hills,

Above the flowery meads, the harvest fields,
The blushing vineyards, 'mid the perilous snows
Where comes not life. Know we not well the snare
Of wealth, the deep retributive pain of sense,
Which ofttimes clog the sad wayfarer's feet
Who treads life's common paths. There are some souls
Too fine and pure to tread them. Were it well
That this brave heart had borne its share of love
And rank and riches, and had lived its life,
Making another's happy in like sort,
And spent its little tale of common days,
And passed and left no sign ? Or was it best
To have touched a high ideal unattained,
To have grown from sufferance to high victory,
To have left the world a story, which shall serve
For ages yet, of soul defeating sense ;
Of aspirations flown too high for earth ;
Of life which spurns the binding chains of love,
And lower weal, and blameless happiness,
And soars aloft and takes the hues of Heaven ? "

And then it was a girl who seemed a youth,
With pure sweet eyes, wearing a monkish garb,
Within whose arms a young child nestled close,
While she along the fields of Paradise
Plucked lilies for it.   Spotless innocence
Shone from her, and around her comely head
A finer motherhood.   And thus the voice :

" In Egypt long ago a humble hind
Lived happy.   One fair daughter of his love
Was his, a modest flower, that came to bless
The evening of his days.   But time and change
Assailed his well-loved home, and took from him
The partner of his life ; and when the blow

Had fallen, loathing of the weary world
Seized him, and, leaving his young girl behind
With some who tended her, he went his way
Across the desert sands, and in a cave
Long time he lived, a pious eremite
Withdrawn from men.   But when the rapid years
Hurried his child to budding maidenhood,
Knowing the perils of the world, his soul
Grew troubled, and he could not bear the dread
That day and night beset him for her sake;
So that his vigils and his prayers seemed vain,
Nor bore their grateful suffrage to the skies,
Since over all his mind would brood a doubt
For her and her soul's health, revolving long
How she should 'scape the world and be with him,
Because no woman might draw near the cell
Of any pious hermit.   At the last
He counselled her, taking the garb of man,
To come to him, leaving the world behind;

And the fair girl, loving her sire, obeyed,
And lived with him in duty to the end.

And when he died, leaving the girl alone,
The brethren of a holy convent near,
Seeing the friendless youth, and pitying
His loneliness, and holding high his love
For his dead sire, offered him food and home
Within the holy house; and there he served,
A young man in the blossom of his age,
Sweet natured, pious, humble, drawing to him
The friendship of the youths, the love of maids.

But all his soul was rapt with thoughts of Heaven,
Taking no thought for earth, and so it came
The youthful Brother grew in every grace
And great humility, and was to all
Example of good life and saintly thought,
And was Marinus to the monks, who loved

Their blameless serving-lad, nor knew at all
That 'twas a maid indeed who lived with them.

Now, as in all humility he served,
The Abbot, trusting him beyond the rest,
Would send him far across the desert sands,
With wagons and with oxen, to the sea,
As steward for the House; and oftentimes
The young man stayed far from his convent home,
With some rude merchant who purveyed their food;
And oft amid the wild seafaring folk
His days were passed, and coarse disordered lives;
And oftentimes the beauty of the youth
Drew many a woman's heart who deemed him man.
But still the saintly tenour of her way
The maiden kept, clothed round with purity,
So that before her face the ribald rout
Grew sober, and among the styes of sense
She walked a saint clothed round with purity,

A youth in grace, keeping a virgin heart.

But one, the daughter of his host, would cast
A loving eye upon him—all in vain ;
For careless still he went his way, nor took
Heed of her love nor her, and oftentimes
He would reprove her of his maiden soul,
Knowing a woman's weakness, and would say,
'Sister, I prithee think of whom thou art,
And set a watch upon thy feet.' But she,
Hating the faithful candour of the youth,
Fell into utter wretchlessness of sin ;
And when her sire, discovering her disgrace,
Threatened her for her fault, a shameless thought
Seized her, and she, with feigned reluctancy,
Sware he deserted her, and with her child
Came to the saintly Abbot, where he sate
Judging the brethren. And great anger seized
The reverend man that at his heart he nursed

A viper which thus stung him, and he cried,
'Vile wretch, who dost disgrace our holy house!
Thou hypocrite, soiling the spotless robe
Of saintly purity! I do denounce
Thy wickedness. No longer canst thou be
A brother to thy brethren here, who live
Pure lives unstained. My sentence on thee is
That thou be scourged, and from this reverend house
Withdraw thyself, and work what viler work
The brethren find for thee; and this poor child
Take thou with thee, and look that thou maintain
Its growing life, since thus thy duty bids thee.
Or if my mercy spare thee from the stripes
Thou hast deserved, 'tis for its sake, not thine.
Go, get thee gone, and never dare again
Pollute my presence.'
     Long she strove to speak,
But her lips formed no word. And then she rose
Meekly, and, answering no word, went forth,

Bowed down with shame, and yet not ill content,
Deeming it but the penance which her sins
Had merited.   And when the little one
Stretched forth its hands, she clasped it to her breast,
Her virgin breast, and all the sacred glow
Of motherhood, which lurks within the hearts
Of innocent maidens, rising soothed her pain ;
And, wandering forth, she found some humble hut
For shelter.   There by alms and servile tasks,
'Mid great despite of all who knew her once
In days of honour ; hungry, lonely, poor,
And ofttimes begging bread, she pined long time,
Till the young life Heaven gave her throve and grew
In happy innocence, and all who passed
Might hear twin voices mingling in the hymns—
The father's, who was mother, and the child's—
And wondering went their way.
                              So that pure soul
Grew tranquil, even on earth.   Yet in her heart

Deep down the rankling sorrow dwelt, and burned
The sources of her being, and sometimes
Her penance grew too hard, and almost broke
The bonds of silence; then again her soul
Took courage, persevering to the end,
Knowing her sins, and how the pain she bore,
Though undeserved, was nothing to the sum
Of her offence, dear heart! and hoping from it
The fair reward of utter faithfulness.

But not the less the insults and the shame
Consumed her life and strength, and day by day,
When now the innocent she loved had grown
To happy childhood, weaker and more weak,
Her failing forces waned, till on her bed
Stretched helpless lay the maid. And when she knew
Her hour was come, she summoned to her side
An agèd woman whom she knew of yore,
What time she seemed a frank and eager youth,
Ere her shame took her; and when she was come,

Quickly with trembling hand she beckoned her,
Giving her charge, when she was dead, to take
Her child to the good brethren, with her prayer
That they should keep it safe.
                         Then with weak hand
She bared her innocent virgin breast and smiled,
A sad wan smile, and, looking up to Heaven,
Breathed her last breath.
                     And she who saw, amazed,
With mingled joy and tears, composed with care
The virgin limbs, and wrapped her in her shroud,
And hasting to the convent with the child
Left orphan, told the tale.   And when he heard,
The holy Abbot knelt with bitter grief
All night before the altar, asking grace
Of Heaven, that he had wronged that saintly soul
By base suspicion; and the brotherhood
Mourned for the pure girl-saint, who bore so long
In blessèd silence taunts and spite and shame,
Obedient and in great humility."

And then it was a saint, still, as it seemed,
Clad in monastic habit,—many a hand
Of painter limns him—with dark beard and hair
And melancholy eyes. Full well I knew
The worn ascetic figure, bearing with it
The lily and the lamb; the tearful gaze
Which wept the sad world's sin, while the high voice
Sang praise for all; the poet-monk who lit
Of his seraphic ardour the faint fires
And embers of the Faith. And thus I heard:

" To wealthy Bernardone and his wife,
Madonna Pica, seven long ages since,
In fair Assisi, on the Umbrian hills,

Was born a son, Giovanni, whom his fellows,
Because he loved the joyous tongue of France,
Would call ' Francesco.' Thence has come a name
Through every Christian realm resounding still,
Beloved for ever, and the ear which hears
' S. Francis of Assisi' knows it takes
A name in which all saintly memories
Are stored as in a precious vase fulfilled
Of spikenard, and the faithful listening soul
Rejoices at the name and is content.

Now, when the boy had come to youthful years,
Being his father's son, rich in all store
Of gay attire, and filled with pride of life
And luxury, yet would his generous heart
Stand at the gate of pity, prompt to give
If any asked ; so that the citizens
Loved the gay, careless youth for all his faults.
Till, when he grew a stripling, a fierce feud

S. Francis of Assisi.

Between Assisi and her sister town
Of high Perugia, raging, burst in war;
And the young Bernardone, with the rest,
Bare arms, and, being taken, twelve long months
Lay prisoner in the fortress.   When the strife
Was done and he set free, the burning grasp
Of fever seized him, and he pined long weeks
And months upon his bed.   There, as he lay
Hovering 'twixt life and death, his sobered thought
Turned oft to Heaven, and all his reckless youth
Stood up accusing, and a great contempt
For this poor fleeting world and all its joys
Filled his reviving life, and crowned his years
With grave and sudden manhood; and he rose
Leaving his former self, a higher hope
Firing his soul than those low aims of yore.

Yet outwardly he kept his wonted use
Of splendour, and among the admiring throng

Of his dear town he seemed to fare as erst
A glittering youth, though 'neath his costly robe
He bore a painful garment, till one day,
Meeting some poor and humble wayfarer,
He knew a noble comrade who had served
With bravery in the war, leading the van
With glory, but whom now some sudden spite
Of Fortune left a beggar. When he saw
The honoured face seamed with the lines of want
And hunger, and the noble form obscured
By rags and penury, the love of God—
Which is the love of man—rose up aflame
Within his breast, and hurriedly he stripped
His broidered velvets from him, clothing round
The naked, as his Lord commanded him,
And with the beggar left his purse, and took
His rags, and through the thronged street passed unmoved,
Rapt by an ecstasy of sacrifice,
And gained his home, a beggar in men's sight,

But wealthy in the love of God and man.

Thence ever in his breast the fire of faith
Burned higher, till one day, within the shrine
Of San Damiano praying, where he mourned
The high church half in ruin ; as he knelt,
There spake within his soul a voice, which said,
' Build thou My falling Church.' And he who heard,
Deeming it was the ruin where he knelt
The strange voice bade him build, turning in haste
To seek his father's house, sold of their store,
And brought the priests the gold. But when his sire
Was angered for the thing, he fled in fear,
Doubting if he had heard the voice aright,
Which bade him build the Church of God indeed,
Not one poor tottering shrine ; and when he came,
After long days, worn, pale, in evil case,
And hungry, all the people deemed the youth
A madman, and his father prisoned him

Within his house long time. But she, his mother,
The mild Madonna Pica, came to him,
And comforted her son, bidding him yield
Obedience to his sire. Yet, though he loved
His gentle mother well, the fire of faith
Burned bright within him, and he spurned the world
And its poor wealth. And when his sire at last,
Being a worldling wholly, summoned him
Before the Bishop, presently his son,
Kneeling before the holy man, flung down
His costly robe, as one who cast away
All worldly wealth, and all the ties of earth,
And gave himself to Heaven. And there he lay
Naked, except his painful vest of hair,
Until the old man, shedding grateful tears
Of tenderness, stooped down and gently raised
The suppliant, and round his limbs he cast
His own white robe ; and thenceforth the young life
Died to the world, and lived for Heaven alone.

S. Francis of Assisi.

Thus the swift years passed by and left him, man,
And turning to the sick and leprous lives,
He spent himself in pity ; and found peace
In happy daily labour, till his soul
Filled with the bliss of living, and his joy
And thankfulness and praise burst forth in song,
As o'er the sunburned Umbrian hills he fared,
He and his chosen Brother, year by year.
Summer and winter, when the high-built town
Glimmered in early dawn, and the thin towers
Gleamed mistlike ; or when now a golden rose
Of sunset woke them, as it wakes to-day
His high arcades, his convent cells, where towers,
Leaving the files of sombre cypress-spires,
Church over church ; or when the valleys slept
In twilight, and the shrill cicale chirped
Among the olives, and the passionate song
Of nightingales, from every bush and grove,

Throbbed liquid through the gloom; then would his voice
Rise clear to Heaven, and these the words he sang:

' Almighty Lord Most High, to Thee belong
Glory and honour, and to none beside;
No soul there is worthy to name Thy Name.

' I praise Thee for Thy creatures, oh my God,
And specially for him who gives us Day,
The Sun, my brother; radiant is his face,
And in his light we see Thy image, Lord.

' I praise Thee, Lord, because Thy hand has made
The Moon, my sister, and the countless host,
In shining mail, which fills the lucid heavens.

' I praise Thee for my brothers, Thy great Winds,
For Air and Cloud, Thy Heavens serene, and all
Thy seasons which give sustenance to men.

'I praise Thee for my sister, the bland force
Of Water, who, to serve the needs of men,
Yields without stint her chaste and precious power.

'I praise Thee for my strenuous brother Fire,
By whose brave aid Thou dost illume the night;
Jocund and fair is he, unquenched and strong.

'I praise Thee for our bounteous mother Earth,
Who keeps and nourishes our race, and gives
A thousand kindly fruits to cheer our lives,
Sweet flowers of varied hues, and every herb.

'I praise Thee for the souls which, for Thy love,
Forgiving evil, sorrow bear and pain;
Blessèd are they who meekly take Thy cross,
And gain, oh Thou Most High! to wear Thy crown.

'I praise Thee for our sister bodily Death,

Whom none who live and breathe shall 'scape at last.
Woe, woe to them who die in mortal sin!
But blest are they, oh Lord, who do Thy Will;
They shall not dread the great, the second Death.

' Thy Name, dear Lord, let all men praise and bless,
And serve Thee still in utter humbleness!'

Thus in an ecstasy of faith he lived,
Begging his bread long time; for all his wealth
He gave to build the churches which he loved,
And in his narrow cell below the hill
On which Assisi towers, hard by the shrine,
Our Lady of the Angels, happy years
He dwelt and pondered, till at length he knew
His mission to the world, to preach, to call
All people to new life, speaking the words
God gave him, not his own. And everywhere
There came a blessing on his work, and men

And pious women listened, and his words
Burned like a fire within their hearts.   And last
Faring to Rome, the Pope, warned in a dream,
Wherein the pilgrim, of his strength, upheld
The tottering Church, gave to his saintly Rule
A blessing; and he turned with joyful heart
To his poor cell, and gathered round him all
His Brethren of the Faith, and there he spent
Long happy years of blessèd Poverty.

Likewise, because for faithful souls the lot
Of God's dumb creatures presses with a weight
Of wonder whence they come, and for what end,
These humble helpers of our race, to whom
Their master is as God, or how the doom
Of nothingness at last awaits their good
And honourable service; and because,
Loving his Lord, he loved all creatures too
His hand had fashioned; worm and creeping thing

Upon his path he crushed not, but would set
In safety; and the joyous songs of birds,
The soaring lark, the passionate nightingale,
He knew for hymns of praise, and oft would join
His jubilant voice with theirs.   Around his feet,
As in the fields he walked, the innocent lambs
Would gambol, and the timid fur-clad things
Nestled within his bosom, fearing not
His gentle hand.   But most of all the birds
He loved, the swift-winged messengers who pass
'Twixt earth and Heaven, and seem as if they bear
A double nature, close in brotherhood
With all he loved; and when he heard their song,
Pierced through with joy and utter thankfulness,
He with alternate praise would join with them,
And once, with soaring antiphons at eve,
Vied with a nightingale, till the brief night
Was well-nigh spent, and he could sing no more,
Since his voice failed him.   And he bade the blithe

Cicale chirping in the acacia thus,
'Sing, sisters; praise the Lord;' and hearing him,
They shrilled their answering song, and he was glad.

And one, the foremost of his band, there was,
The Lady Clara, then and now a saint.
She with the Master lived in grave discourse
And holy converse, and one day it seemed,
When at their frugal meal upon the grass
She, with her sisters, sate around the saint,
He with such sweet discourse declared the Faith,
That they forgot their food and paused to take
The spiritual feast, with eyes and hearts
Raised up to Heaven; and all the folk around
Marked how the convent and the low church gleamed
With light which shone like fire, and, hasting there,
Found the saints wrapt in silent musing thought,
Forgetful of their meal, and knew the light
Was but the fire divine of Faith, which burned

Within those saintly hearts, and to their homes
Turned wondering.

              But while he lived serene,
Dissolved in happy tears, his soul desired
The martyr's blessèd palm, and fain would go
Forth to the Paynim host, which then bore rule
O'er all the sacred fields of Palestine;
But a storm drove him back. Then to the Moor
He yearned to preach; but grievous sickness came,
And stayed his feet. Last, by the fabulous Nile,
He gave his body to burn if they would take
The Faith of Christ; but when the Moslem heard,
Deeming such sacrifice too great for man,
He sent him home with honour. Not for him
The martyr's palm, but to build up the Church
By years of labour crowned with saintly death.

Thus ten years passed, and then upon the plain
Around his cell the Brethren of his Rule

In thousands flocked from every Christian land,
And by his triple Vow of Poverty,
Obedience, Chastity, bound fast their lives,
As the saint bade them, and to every clime
Went forth his envoys. He it was who first,
A rapt ascetic, with foreseeing mind,
Brought to the service of the Faith the lives
Whose path lay through the world, and the fresh zeal
Of Woman, from the peasant to the Queen.
Long from his place he governed far and wide
His nascent order, till at last, his soul
Grown sick for Heaven and heavenly thoughts, he passed,
Far from his brethren and the praise of men,
To some lone cell on the precipitous side
Of blue Alverno, high above the vale,
Above the winding river, above the heights
Of white Assisi, where his failing sight
Might rest upon the everlasting hills.
There, in rapt contemplation and fair dreams,

He spent his soul.

                There, year by rapturous year,
The heavens stood open to his gaze ; the face
Of the Madonna, with the Child Divine,
Beamed on him. There the blessèd Presence filled
His yearning eyes. There, in an ecstasy
'Twas said, the failing body, strong in love,
And the pure soul cleansed from her earthy stains,
Took his dear Master's wounds, and bore again
The Passion ; and the inmost Heaven, unsealed,
Opening disclosed the Angelic Host and all
The glories else unseen by mortal eye,
Till, in seraphic ardour, the saint's soul,
Throbbing with bliss well-nigh too great for earth,
Wore thin the walls of life, and sickness came,
And weakness, and his eyes grew dim with tears—
Tears not of sorrow all, but mixt with joy
For those his happy visions ; tears of pain
For the world's sin ; tears of a faithful hope

For Heaven and all the blessedness to be.

There, when he knew his end draw nigh, he hailed
The coming freedom; and, because his soul
Was humble, ordered that his bones should rest
Where, mouldering in unconsecrated ground,
The malefactors lay. Then, with weak voice,
Bidding them set him on the sweet bare earth
Beneath the evening sky, he murmured low
The Imploring Psalm, 'To Thee, Lord, have I cried;
Thou art my hope;' and struggling to the close,
'Bring my soul out of prison,' straightway breathed
His last pure breath.
     Then those who loved him bare
His body to the tomb. And when they passed
By San Damiano, all the sorrowing nuns,
S. Clara and her sisters, weeping, knelt
And kissed his hands; and that dishonoured grave,
Since there a saint slept in the peace of Heaven,

Grew honoured for all time and consecrate.

And over him they built a stately church,
Wherein, beneath a costly pillared shrine
Of jasper and of sardonyx, he waits,
Who was so poor in life, the Judgment Day,
And named it by his name; and there, hard by,
They reared a stately convent of his Rule;
And church and convent, of the loving skill
Of painters whom the Faith's reviving fire
Kindled to Art, glow with celestial hues
Of beauty. There the archaic simple hand
Of Cimabue wrought. There Giotto dreamt
His saintly stories, only part of earth,
While the stern Bard of Heaven and Hell stood near
With counsel, honouring the name he deemed
' A sunrise on the world.' There, quaintly true,
Orcagna, Cavallini, Gozzoli,
Light the rich walls. There blooms the stainless thought

Of the Angelic Brother, and the pure
Rapture of Perugino, and the soul
He reared, the wonder and despair of Art,
Raffaelle, and a throng of names inspired
Who sought not fame of men. And compassed round
By those high glories lies the sacred dust
Of him who, wedding saintly Poverty,
Lived there long time despised, though now he soars
Higher than earthly thrones, a Saint in Heaven."

Next came a queenly, youthful figure, clad
In the Franciscan garb, a slender form
With dark-brown hair and eyes, whose lap was filled
With roses white and red, like those which crowned,
In token of her purity and love,
The brow of Cecily.   Great tenderness
And pity beamed from out her saintly eyes,
And, kissing as she went her stainless robe,
Knelt many a soul her faithful voice and hand
Had raised from earth to heaven.   As she came
This fair half-legendary tale I heard:

" To Andreas of Hungary the Queen,
His consort, seven long centuries ago,

Bore one fair daughter. All the realm that year
Was free from war, a bounteous harvest blessed
The peaceful land, and with her birth a saint
To bless the Church of God.
                    From her first years
Saintly she showed and meek; no childish tear
Of petulance she shed, and when she spake
Her speech was as a prayer. All the broad plain
Of Hungary rejoiced to see her grow
As wise as fair, and through the land the fame
Of her young goodness spread and made men glad.

Now, when King Herman, of Thuringia, learned
This prodigy, he sent an embassy
To Hungary to ask of Andreas
His daughter in betrothal for his son
Prince Lewis, and the messengers returned
And brought the child with them, and, with her, store
Of costly stuffs and jewels the far East

And rich Byzantium yielded. And the King
Loved the child well, and with her love she lived,
Brother and sister; and her youthful heart
Was filled with Heaven, and every day that came
Brought its fair tale of saintly sacrifice,
And more and more for God and in His fear
She lived her girlish life, filling her days
With pity and compassion, till she showed
As 'twere some sweet child-angel whom the hand
Of a great painter limns. Not as a child
Of this poor trivial world she seemed, but grave,
As one who strayed from Heaven to earth and found
No meet companion. But the Prince loved well
His young betrothed, albeit well he saw
She was not as the rest, fearing sometimes
Lest she might choose to be the Bride of Heaven,
And not for him. Yet, while the good King lived,
None dared to thwart the young Elizabeth
In any work of pity, nor might the tooth

Of envy touch her.   But when death cut short
His life, the stranger, now a friendless maid,
Dwelt long forlorn, because the jealous Queen
And her proud daughter Agnes, envying
Her saintly life, with scoffs and jeers would mock
Her sacrifice, and deepest contumely,
So that her young and modest soul would shrink
Within her at the cruel daily taunts
Which marred her life ; and all the courtly throng
Marked her disgrace, and mocked her ; and her sister,
The Princess Agnes, jealous of her love,
Would wring her heart, declaring that her brother
Wanted no nun for bride, but would dismiss her
To Hungary in shame.   Such rankling shafts
Of venom launched they as the poisoned tongue
Of envious women can ; and she, alone,
Unfriended, bare it, nor complaining word
Would speak to her betrothed, who marked it all
In silence, nor yet spake, being indeed

A youth as yet in tutelage, who owed
Obedience to the Queen, doubting, maybe,
Within his inmost heart if this pure soul
Were not too high for earth and earthly love.

But not the less his faithful love and trust
Sustained her soul. No public word he spake
Of comfort, but ofttimes, when she would sit
In tears within her chamber, sick at heart
For the despite and all the contumely
The others showered on her, her youthful lover
Would come to her, comforting her with words;
And when they were apart, his faithful thought
Fixed on her still, he, coming, brought with him
Some little gift she loved—a rosary
Of beads, a silver crucifix, a chain
Of gold in token of his love. And she,
Loving him next to Heaven, would dry her tears
And run to meet him, and throw girlish arms

Around him, and would strain him to her heart
And take his kisses as a maiden should
Who loves and is beloved, and with good heart
And cheerful bear her cross, nor cease at all
From works of mercy, trusting to her love.

Now one day, as it chanced, her lover went
With neighbouring princes to the chase, and stayed
Longer than was his wont, and when he came,
Or over-tired or busied with his guests,
Brought not his wonted gift, nor did embrace
His love with kisses; and the jealous throng
Marked him; and she, perceiving with what joy
They saw his coldness, found her fainting heart
Sink in her, and she sent a messenger
Who should enquire of Lewis and his love.
And when he came, he found the weary Prince
Lying at rest; and when he asked of him
If he still loved the Princess, for the throng

Had marked his coldness; springing to his feet,
The Prince replied, 'Seest thou yon lofty hill
Which towers above us? If it were of gold
From base to peak, pure gold, Heaven be my witness,
I would give it all for her. I love none other.
I must have my Elizabeth; I love her
Better than all the world.' And then he drew
A little silver mirror from his purse,
Wrought deftly, with an image of the Lord,
And sent it her for gage; and when the maid
Took it, she kissed with joy and reverence
The sacred image, doubting him no more
Till they were wed—he a tall, vigorous youth,
Of ruddy cheek, blue eyes, and royal port,
And in his speech as modest as a maid;
And she a budding maiden, dark of hair
And eye, the large dark eye, which always glowed
With inward light of love and charity,
And which great pity for the labouring world

Ofttimes impearled with tears.
                         And so long time
They lived together in happy wedded love.
But she, within her royal cloister, still
Kept her old penances, and oft at night
She left her husband while he slept, and knelt
On the cold ground, and oftentimes she scourged
Her tender flesh; and he, who loved her dear,
Would chide her, but in vain. Yet none the less
She did fulfil her lofty courtesies,
And rode out with him to the chase, and showed
A Queen for all to see. Though when he went
She donned a mourning weed, when he returned
She, in her royal mantle clad, would greet
Her spouse, and would embrace him as he leapt
Down from his charger, every inch a Queen,
Greeting her lord with wifely tenderness;
Yet when they sat at meat, 'twas bread alone
They served to her, and in her cup they poured

Not wine, but water only, till her spouse
Tasting the cup one day, it seemed to him
The water of her saintly penance glowed
Like some celestial wine pressed from the grapes
Of Paradise, and not a word he spake,
Because he held long time his wife was served
By angel hands and fed on angels' food.

And one day, when her lord had made a feast
For all his brother princes, filled with pride
Of his fair wife, and willing that his peers
Should judge her beauty, he gave charge to her
That, clothed in costly robes, a Queen to see,
She should attend the feast; and she, who held
Obedience more than all, arrayed herself
In queenly garb. Upon her raven hair
She set a glittering diadem of gems,
And round her shapely form a royal robe
Of green and gold, and o'er her fair neck threw

An ermined mantle.   As she issued forth
From out her queenly bower to join her lord,
Behold, a hapless beggar, spent with cold
And hunger, met her, asking charity;
And when he prayed her, in the sacred Name,
To succour him, she, with the holy fire
Of pity rising in her, stripped from her
The ermine, and around the shivering form
Wrapped it, and went, half doubting if her spouse
Would pardon her.   And when he came, she ran
And, leaning on his bosom, told him all;
And while he stood irresolute, behold,
Her maiden with the mantle in her arms.
'Madam, I found your ermine in its place;
Why did your Highness leave it?'   Then she clasped it
Around her; and her husband, as he heard,
Knew well the beggar was the Lord of all;
Willing to test her love and charity;
And they together went; and all the guests

Marvelled to see her beauty—such a light
Shone from her jewelled mantle, and her head
Seemed set with glory, and her tender eyes
Lit with the glow of Heaven and saintly love.

And one day, when she toiled amidst her poor
At Eisenach, she came upon a child
Outcast of all, because a loathly plague
Of leprosy possessed him, so that none
Would touch him. Straight she took him in her arms,
Moved by a holy pity, and up the steep
Carried him to her castle, while the throng
Of courtiers shrank from her, and in her bed
Laid him, and tended him with saintly love,
Despite the old Queen's anger, all unmoved.
And when her lord returned, and they would tell him
What they had seen, he hurried to the place,
Half in disgust, and snatched the coverlet
Aside; and, lo! no leper child was there,

Only the childish radiant form which lay
Within the manger once at Bethlehem;
And as they gazed the lovely vision smiled
And faded, and was gone.
      Again, one day,
When to her work she issued forth alone
In winter down the snows, and in her robe,
To feed the hungry, doles of meat and bread,
Upon the frozen path she chanced to meet
Her husband, and in jest he greeted her.
'What dost thou here, my Elsbeth, and what store
Lies hid within thy cloak?' Then, with a blush
Of modesty divine, which lit her face
With double beauty, she drew close her robe,
Lest he should see. But he, with frolic mirth
Persisting, drew it back, and in the fold
He seemed to see, amid those wintry snows,
Celestial roses red and white, which breathed
A fragrance not of earth; and when he sought

To clasp her to his breast, lo! from her eyes
An awful radiance shone, too bright for earth;
And, bidding her go forward on her way,
One heavenly bloom he took, and next his heart
He laid it, and, with head declined, and slow,
And pondering much, climbed to their royal home.

.

In such good works she spent her saintly life.
When famine vexed the people, and her lord
Was with his liege far off, she opened wide
The royal granaries to save, unasked,
Those starving lives; and when the pestilence,
A dread familiar following in its train,
Seized them, her hand it was that smoothed the bed
Of sickness, rearing costly hospices
For all, but chiefly for the helpless lives
Of children. When she walked among the throng,
A tall young queenly figure breathing grace,
The little ones would cling to her and lisp

The sacred name of mother; and she stooped
And cherished them, speaking with homely words
Of comfort, and for them she sold her robes,
Her gems, and all the precious things she loved,
Nay, even the jewels of the State. And he
Returning, when they came and made complaint
Of all she lavished, with a smile would say,
' Nay, is my dear wife well, and are they well,
My children? Ay? Then it is well with me.
If she but spare my castle, it is well;
Let her give alms.' And she, with all her brood,
Came forth and flung her on his breast, and kissed
Her love, and welcomed him with tender words—
'See, I have given the Lord what is His own,
And He preserves us these.'

Thus sped their wedded lives, till the sad year
When, the third time, the armies of the Cross
Sailed forth to fight the Crescent. At their head

The Kaiser went, leading the princely throng,
And Lewis with them. And the brave man feared
One thing alone, to see his sorrowing wife
Blanch at the news. Therefore the Cross he took
Not on his breast he bore, but carried it
Hid safe from prying eyes, because he dared not
Witness her pain. But one fair summer eve,
As they together sate within her bower,
Asking of him an alms for some good end,
Which he in jest denied, she with blithe heart
Snatched his purse from him, and beheld within
The Cross, and straight, knowing what thing it was,
Swooned at his feet; and when her life returned,
Weeping, she said, 'Dear husband, stay with me
If God so will;' and he, dissolved in tears:
'Dear wife, I dare not; I am vowed to Heaven.'
Then she: 'God's will be done.' And so he went;
And she a two days' journey fared with him
Ere she could say 'Farewell,' nor saw her eyes

Her love again on earth; for when he reached
The far Calabrian shore, some swift disease
Seized him, and to the nobles round his bed
Commending his loved wife and children dear,
Within the Patriarch's arms the Landgrave died.

And she, when now the news of her lost love
Came to her, swooned away, and lay for dead
Long time, and at the last, a broken heart,
Tending her infant brood, she bore to live;
But when her shield, her stay, her strong support
Was taken from her, then she 'gan to prove
The vile despite they know who find the world,
The ungrateful world, scorning their feebleness.
From her proud castle home they drove her forth,
Her and her children, and, amid the snows
Of winter, down the rocky steep they went,
A sad procession. In her arms the Queen
Folded her suckling child, born when his sire

Was dying far away, and with her went
Three faithful ladies, bearing each a child,
Seeking some hind's poor hut; and as they went
Down the rough slippery way, her weary feet
Stumbling, upon the ground she lay, and then
A thing in shape of woman, whom her hand
Tended through sickness, mocked her as she fell.
Yet not the less her sweet and patient spirit
Was all unmoved to wrath; and, having found
Some humble shelter, day by day she wrought
At spinning for her children, whom her skill
Furnished with food and clothing, till the knights
From the Crusade returning, set her boy
Upon his father's throne, and gave to her
Marbourg for dower, where with her girls she dwelt
Long unmolested.   But a pitiless man,
Conrad the priest, within whose bigot soul
Pity nor mercy dwelt; whether to make

Her life one penance, that he might increase
His baleful power o'er that pure heart, or else
Wishing to set her name among the saints,
And his the honour, laid upon her soul
Penance too hard to bear. He took from her
Her children one by one, lest too much love
Might hinder her from Heaven. He took from her
The one delight of giving, which grows strong
With waning life; and when she fain would take
The vows of San Francesco, and would beg
Her bread throughout the world, this too forbade;
And when, with clothing torn and things of shreds,
She, who was once a queen, through her own town
Wandered, the children of her loving care
Mocked her as one demented. Yet she bore
All this and worse, meek and without complaint,
Until the pious seemed to see once more
The lowly Clara and revered a saint.

Yet worse than all her unearned penances,
The tooth of slander would invade her peace;
And she, the saintly lady whose white life
Was all of Heaven, leaving within the grave
All earthly love, knew as a worldling might
The breath of shame—she whose fair delicate flesh
Was scarred with lashes which the fanatic rage
Of the dark bigot wreaked on her. And yet
Her cup of suffering was not full; but last
The dark priest took from her the faithful hearts
Who, knowing her in honour, were content
To cleave to her disgrace, and in their stead
Sent two base creatures, who should make her drain
Dishonour to the dregs, forbidding her
The alms she loved, or that which was indeed
Her second nature—her unsparing work
Among the poor and sick. No marvel then
That, ere her morning broadened into noon,

Her great compassion, languishing and pent
Like an undying fire within her soul,
Burned with a quenchless longing, and consumed
Her tender youth, which all her pains and stripes,
The scourge of slander, nay, her dead love's loss,
Slew not; or that her life, laid on a bed
Of suffering, day by day waned low and lower,
Nor ever again revived, but sank at last
In that thick darkness which we christen Death.

And when upon her bed she came to die,
Being but four and twenty summers old,
When she had lain twelve days or more, they heard
Who tended her, a sweet and soaring strain
Sound from her lips, as to the wall she turned
Her wasted face. All her last day on earth
She strove in prayer, till by the mystic food
Her listening ear, enfranchised, seemed to hear
Voices of angels, and the Mother of God

In converse with her, and the sound of hymns
Sweeter than any sounds of earth ; and last,
When now her strength had failed, one word she spake :
'Silence !'—no more, as one who fain would hear
The heavenly quires ; and then she made response,
'Contempsi regnum mundi Domine.'
And then the voices ceased, and she with them
Closed her pure saintly life.

      And round her bed
The people gathered, mourning, bathed in tears.
Four days she lay unburied in the midst,
While the crowd knelt and kissed.

        And on the site
Of her poor home they reared the stately Church
Of S. Elizabeth, and her shrine within,
Built high on steps worn hollow by the knees
Of countless pilgrims ; till the gathering storm
Of revolution burst, and violated
Those sacred walls, and one of her own blood,

The Landgrave Philip, came with reckless hand
And razed the shrine, and scattered far and wide
The relics of the saint ; and no man knows
Their resting-place, but her soul rests with God."

Thus he ; and then, with graver thought and voice,
My soul within me burst in words and cried,
" ' Be good, be good !'—this is the word that Heaven
Proclaims, not 'happy ;' or if happiness
Come, 'tis despite the pain the careless world
Wreaks upon finer souls. Here there is strife,
Injustice, suffering, and the cruel sense
Of failure, when the victor's palm, indeed,
Is theirs to claim. Death comes and takes our lives
With half our work undone, and Faith itself
Breeds its own errors and misguides the soul,
And all our happiness seems sunk in night,
Till the Great Dawn arising brings with it
New heavens and new earth."

                              Then a form meek
And pitiful, in manhood's early prime,
With mild soft eyes, who wore the pilgrim's garb,
The scallop in his hat, the staff, the scrip,
The wallet, and yet seemed a noble still
For all his poverty; and my guide said—

" In Languedoc, of noble parents came,
When thirteen centuries were passed from Christ,
A youth, who bore upon his breast from birth,
Symbol of dedication to the Faith,
A tiny cross. Him with all pious care
His mother, Libera, for works of good
And sanctity, through all his glowing youth,

Trained year by year; and on his soul he bore
The cross, as on his breast, and gave his life,
His heart, his all, to Heaven.
     But not with him
The pale ascetic fervours of the cell,
Nor cloistered virtues lived apart from men,
Where the rapt soul communes alone with God,
Prevailed; but life lived as his Master's erst,
Among the poor and weak, healing the sick,
And filled with pity for the fallen lives
Of sinners, raising them to light and hope—
Life spending happy, and laborious days,
Each bringing something of accomplished good,
And sinking at its close in well-earned rest;—
'Twas this blest lot he prized.
      Thus, all his youth
He lived in innocence. But ere he reached
The gate of early manhood, Death, which comes
To rich and poor, took from him at a blow

His father's guiding hand, his mother's prayers,
And he, an orphan, rich in lands and gold,
Was left to work what work was his, alone.

Then with no pause of doubt, knowing the words
Of his dear Master, and remembering well
His answer to the youth who, rich as he,
Would fain obey, straightway he gathered all
His wealth, and of it to the poor and weak
Gave part in alms, and of the rest he reared
Hospices for the sick, wherein the skill
Of wise physicians, working under Heaven,
Might heal them; and he donned a pilgrim's garb,
And then on foot, obscure, like any hind,
Painful with staff and wallet toiled to Rome.

But when his feet had left the Alpine snows,
Crossing the Lombard plain, one eve, he climbed,
Through groves of oak, to where, its slender towers

S. Roch.

Dark on the twilight glow, throbbing with noise
Of loud-tongued waters hurrying to the plain,
By Orvieto's city and sacred shrine,
Acquapendente hung.   But as he came,
The nameless dread of some invisible ill,
The unguarded city gates, the tolling knells,
The sick and dying cumbering the ways
With none to aid, the still, deserted streets,
The sullen silence echoing cries of pain
From the blind, close-shut dwellings, smote on him
With a strange pity, and he hastened on.
And when he asked of one who fled, what ill
Befell the town, "The plague!" he cried, "the plague!
Fly too, or thou art doomed."   But he who heard,
Without a moment's doubt, filled with great ruth
And eagerness, pressed onward, as a player
Who knows and loves his part, and round his feet
Dread signs of death and suffering everywhere
Grew thicker, till at length he gained the gate

Of the great hospice, thronged from floor to roof
With hopeless pain.   Then, in an ecstasy,
He entered, and besought that he might serve ;
And they consenting, he, with fervent prayer
And great compassion, and the finer skill
Which Faith can breed, and comfortable words,
And signing with the Cross where'er he came,
Heartened those helpless sufferers in such sort
That many, whom now the instant might of Death
Held in its grasp, escaped ; and presently,
The fierce infection waning, all the land
Revered the youth, so young, so beautiful,
So fearless and devoted, and they grew
To hold him more than man, till to their thought
He showed as 'twere an angel sent from Heaven
To bid them live.

     Thence fared he through the land
Of the Romagna.   There by field and town
Was pestilence, and he was in the midst,

S. Roch.

Dauntless amid the harm, tending the sick,
Himself unscathed.   And thence to Rome herself,
Where too was plague; there three long years he wrought,
'Mid scenes of death and pain, tending the sick,
Always unscathed, and wheresoe'er he went
A blessing went with him upon his work.

Yet one incessant prayer his faithful lips
Would breathe to Heaven, if only he might earn
The martyr's palm : but never at all there came
An answer to his prayer, nor could he die,
Nor be at rest, for God had need of him.

Thus, year by year, from town to suffering town
He journeyed, still unscathed, rapt by good works
Of mercy.   At the last his footsteps came
To fair Piacenza, where a dreadful ill
Consumed the people.   There long time he served,
Tending the sick.   There, too, a blessing came

Upon his work, till one sad night he sank,
O'ercome by toil and watching, on the ground;
And when he woke, a burning fever raged
Through every vein, and on his breast, behold,
A horrible tumour. Then, because his pain
Had grown too great for silence, and he feared
To wake the suffering sleepers, he crawled forth
And laid him down to die; and when the guard,
Fearing the plague, constrained him, slowly crept,
Tottering in pain, upon his pilgrim's staff,
Beyond the city gates, to a thick wood
Where no man came, and there prepared to die.

But not yet came his Fate, for some poor hind
Succoured him, and would dress his wound and bring
His daily food, or, as some tell, there came
A bright angelic form to comfort him,
And he was healed; and when his strength returned,
Exulting in his soul that he was found

S. Roch.

Worthy to suffer for his Lord, and filled
With holy pride, he rose and took his way
Across the swelling Apennines, the plains,
The Alpine snows, clad in his pilgrim's garb,
A worn and weary man, bent by long toil
And wan from mortal sickness, till he gained
His own fair native land; and to a town
Which was his own, and all the country folk
His vassals born, he came, so changed and bent
By long and suffering years, no living eye
Knew him, and 'midst the people who were his
The pilgrim walked unknown who was their lord.

And he, because he scorned to take again
His lordly rank, but rather chose to be
In great humility and serve unknown
The suffering race of men, would speak no word
Of recognition, but, a stranger still,
Passed through the country side, nor claimed his own,

Loving the saintly poverty which brought
His soul to God, and set him free to move
Lowly amongst the lowly, doing good.

Then, since great strifes and bitter jealousies
Vexed all the country side, the folk who deemed
His pilgrim's robe no other than a cloak
To hide the traitor, haled him to the judge,
His father's brother. No defensive word
He spoke, nor knew his kinsman, whom he doomed
To lifelong prison. And the pilgrim, glad
Of salutary pain, and holding all
Was of God's will—the judge's ignorance
Of his own blood, and all his punishment—
Kept silence till the end, and to his cell
And chains went silently, who for a word
Had been set free with honour. There he pined,
In a close dungeon pent, long weary years,
Leaving his fate to Heaven.

S. Roch.

                And when his hour
Was come, the jailor, taking to his cell
His bread and water, found the prisoner lie
Dead on his pallet, and around his head
And from his wasted face a glory shone
Which lit the gloom, and by his side a scroll,
Writ by what hand none knew: "Whoever dreads
The pestilence that stalketh through the night
Shall seek the intercession of the saint
Who lies here dead—Roch, Lord of Languedoc."

Then in a moment, looking on the face
Of the worn pilgrim-prisoner dead and cold,
They knew again the ardent, generous youth
Who, gay with robes of price and gems and gold,
In the first bloom of manhood, beamed on them
And gave up all for Heaven, and tender ruth
For dim afflicted lives whom the hard fate
Of hopeless sickness took.   And so their eyes

Were opened, and the judge, his kinsman, wept
His hapless fate, stricken with a deep remorse
For what had been; and, touched with vain regret,
His vassals laid him in a costly tomb
With tears and lamentations; and they thought
That from the sacred relics of the dead,
As when he lived, there went a virtue forth
In plague and sickness, so that still he seemed
To heal them.   And when now a century passed,
The strong sons of the Mistress of the seas,
Who languished oft beneath the dreadful scourge
The seething Orient bred, sailed out and snatched
His sacred dust, and forth, with pious care
And honour, all the fairy city came
To meet them; and above him, presently,
They reared a church in honour of the saint,
San Rocco, and a pitiful Brotherhood,
Named by his name, to aid the poor and sick,

Wherein the proudest noble joyed to serve—
The Scuola di San Rocco,—and a house
Stately as any which the enchanted sea
Exhales in dreaming Venice. There the skill
Of Tintoretto and his scholars limned
On wall and ceiling stories of our Lord,
His Death, and his Ascension to the skies,
With lavish hand, so that it glows to-day
A miracle of Art, which fitly frames
A statue of the saint; and there he stands,
As stands his soul, among the heavenly host,
In honour now, who died a prisoner here."

Next 'twas a woman, bearing in her hand
A lily.   Round her maiden limbs she drew
The habit of S. Dominic.   Her worn face
Bore anxious traces still, as that of one
Whom, loving best the cloister, the sad world
Calls to its service and denies to Heaven;
And I bethought me of a cloudless noon
By Fonte Branda, 'mid the merry talk
Of thirsty peasants, while the churches towered
High on the rocky spurs, and her low home
Showed like a sacred shrine, where the saint once
Doubted herself, not God.   And thus the voice:

" In fair Siena, on the Tuscan hills,

Giacomo Benincasa lived and died
Five centuries ago. To him were born,
And his wife Lapa, many stalwart sons
And fair-grown daughters. One, their dearest child,
Was Catharine, latest born and best beloved,
So fair, so blithe, so sweet in infancy,
The neighbours named her name Euphrosyne.

But as she grew, no longer the young maid
Showed as her comrades, but the world unseen
Made grave her gaze and checked the innocent flow
Of girlish laughter, and the pictured tales
Of saintly lives within the incensed gloom
Of the great churches drew her childish feet
With a strange charm. For one day, as she came,
Being but seven summers in the world,
She and her brother, from some natal feast,
They sate at sunset on the rocky hill
By Fonte Branda, and as Catharine gazed

On the tall campanile of the church
Above her, lo! beyond the slender shaft,
The heavens stood open, and her wondering gaze
Saw our dear Lord in glory, and the saints
Around Him. As she looked upon the sight
In ecstasy, her eyes grew fixed, and she
Gazed on, unconscious that her brother's voice
Called to unheeding ears; and when he turned
And drew her from her place, she saw no more
The opened heavens, and, sobbing from her heart,
Sank on the ground with bitter childish tears.

Nor ever from her thought the wondrous dream
Of that blest evening faded. More and more
Silent she grew, and grave, and wandered forth
In solitude, if haply once again
That glorious vision took her longing eyes;
But never more it came. But she, who read
The tale of Catharine and the sponsal ring

Which bound her to the Lord, prayed if perchance
She also might be His; and when she came
To her full age, being sweet and beautiful,
Her parents, loving not her penances,
Her fasts, her vigils, her ascetic dreams,
Would give their girl in marriage; but her soul,
Fixed on that heavenly bridal, took no thought
For earthly love, and still her days were spent
In solitary prayer.   Then, that hard toil
Might check her wandering dreams, her parents laid
Hard household tasks upon her, loading her
With mean and weary toils, and all the house
Mocked her and jeered; but in her heart she kept
This comfort—'Were not, then, the blessèd saints
Mocked even as I, and shall I be ashamed
To bear as they did?'   To her humble tasks
She bent her unrepining; food and rest
Almost she took not, yielding place to prayer;
And, lest her fairness might allure the eyes

Of youthful lovers, from her shapely head
Sheared the luxuriant treasure of her hair,
To lay before the altar, offering all
Her youth, her life to Heaven. Thus she lived
A recluse self-ordained; but still her sire
Urged her to wed, till one day, to her cell
Chancing to come, it seemed a snow-white dove
Hovered above her as she knelt, and then
The good man, fearing lest his will withstood
The Spirit which thus visibly guided her,
Entreated her no more, leaving her free
To do Heaven's will. And to the holy house
Of Dominic she went, and there she sought
To serve, a penitent, but never yet
Made full profession, though she found no less
A penance for herself. On a bare board
She lay, a log her pillow, and no word
For three long years she spake; but from her cell
High in her father's roof, with earliest dawn,

And when the darkening ways grew dim with night,
Daily she climbed the steep where the tall Church
Of San Domenico towered, by whose thin shaft
She saw Heaven opened once, and there she knelt
Before the altar rapt in ecstasy.

But not yet found she peace or rest, for still
The Enemy of Man spread for her snares
To take her fast. Thoughts sent he to her soul
Like fiery darts, thoughts which she deemed of sin,
Such as assailed the blessèd Anthony.
Or was it, surely, that to this white life
The dreams of blameless love, and hearth and home,
And the soft hands of children at the breast,
Seemed perilous for ill? But when they came,
She prayed anew for help, she took not food,
She scourged herself before the altar-place
Till her blood flowed. And when she called for aid
At midnight in the lonely church, she seemed

To see a visible Presence walk with her,
Speak to her words of sweetness, comfort her
As One alone might comfort, flood her soul
With faith, till, as she walked, the darkling aisles
Glowed with warm light, and the chill pavement smiled
Decked with sweet summer flowers; and evermore
The gracious accents of a voice Divine,
Filling her ears, made precious melody,
Waking the ghostly solitude with sound,
And blessèd faces bent, and blest hands swept
Celestial lyres unseen.   And then sometimes
They came not, nor the Presence, and her soul
Fainted within her, lest those heavenly dreams
Were nought but snares, unreal fantasies
Sent of the enemy to take her soul—
The dreams which bind the saintly dreamer fast
(Like siren voices sounding o'er the sea,
Which whoso heard, nor fled nor stopped his ears,
Lay bound for ever and lost); nor ever again

The healthful daily load of duty done
Allures, nor honest toil, who pines in chains
Self-forged, a prisoner to his brooding thought.

And so she turned from penance and from fast
And blessèd contemplation to the tasks
Of Christian duty. To the poor and weak
She lived a servant. One poor wretch there was,
Sick of a hopeless ill. For her she bore
Through wintry nights, on her bent back, the load
Of fuel for her fire. Another, white
With leprosy, she succoured where she lay
Houseless without the walls. In her own bed
She laid and tended her, till on her hands
The hopeless evil showed. Yet nought she earned
Of gratitude, and when the leper died,
She only, and none other, durst prepare
Her corpse for burial; and, behold, her hurt
Was cleansed from that same hour! And on a day

When from the town she went on some soft task
Of mercy, through the city gates there came
A sad procession; for a robber went
Forth to his shameful doom, rending the air
With blasphemies and wild despairing cries,
While in his wake the angry people surged
With curses; and her tender saintly heart
O'erflowed with pity, and she took her place
Beside him, speaking with such gracious words
That his hard heart was melted, and confessed
His heinous sin and its just punishment.
And while she knelt in prayer, forgetting all,
Lo! the poor penitent, 'like a gentle lamb,'
Went tranquil to his death, and she who saw,
Calling him 'her sweet brother,' laid his head
Upon the block; and when the keen axe fell,
She sate, his severed head within her hands,
All bathed in precious blood, while her rapt eyes
Saw the saved soul borne upward into heaven.

In such fair works of love the virgin saint
Spent her pure days, till through the land her fame
Spread far and wide ; and when the Florentines
Grew rebels to the Church, the Pontiff named her
Arbitress of the strife, confiding to her
The terms of peace. But when she made her way
To Florence, straight a tumult, and she hid,
Learning too soon how base the ingrate throng,
Within the cloister. 'Twas her voice which called
The Holy Father home, her woman's voice—
None other. Weighty matters of the State
Were hers to adjudge, untrammelled, as she would ;
So that the visionary girl of yore
Rose to the stately woman, ruling well,
As might a Queen, in honour and fame of men.

But in the midst of all the pomp, the glare
Of rank and power, still would her yearning gaze

Steal backward to the days, now long ago,
When painfully at midnight up the steep
Her feet would climb, and in the towering church
Pour out her innocent soul, and feel the breath
Of Love Divine upon her cheek, and walk
Encompassed round with Heaven and the fair dreams
Which could defy the morning and waxed strong
Even in the blaze of noon; and she would prize
The contemplative life, the silent thought,
Which there she knew, above the clamorous din
And turmoil of the world, the hopes, the fears,
The slanderous tooth of secret enmity,
The envy of false friends. And so deep care,
Chafing the thin-worn vesture of her life,
Laid her at last upon her bed, and broke,
Before her footsteps trod life's middle way,
The silver cord, and loosed her soul to Heaven.

But as she lay upon her bed and knew

Her end drew near, one word she spoke alone—
'Nay, Lord, 'twas not vainglory, as they say,
That drew me, but Thine honour, and Thine alone;
And thou, Lord, knowest this it was, not pride.'
And so she passed away."

     But when his voice
Was silent, all my soul broke forth in words
Of Love which conquered Doubt.
       "Dear spotless soul,
Still through thy house men go, and wondering mark
Thy place of prayer, thy chamber, and thy cell.
Here 'twas the Lord appeared, and gave to thee
His sacred heart. Here, in this very spot,
Thou clothedst Him as He sate in rags and seemed
A beggar. All the house is filled with thee
And the white simple story of thy life;
Still, far above, the high church on the hill

Towers where, in prayer, thou seemedst to walk wrapt
    round
By an ineffable Presence; thy low roof
Is grown as 'twere a shrine, where priest and nun
And visionary girls from age to age
Throng and repeat the self-same prayers, thyself
Didst offer year by year.
                      Comes there no end
Of yearning for our race on earth, nor stay
Of penance, nor unmingled happiness
Till Heaven is gained? or in high Heaven itself
Can fancy image, or can faith sustain,
No shadow, nor satiety of joy?
I cannot tell, I know not, but I know
'Tis not for happiness we are, but God."

George Herbert.

And then I saw a reverend figure come,
Walking with meditative steps and slow,
Who listened as the blest Cecilia erst
To high celestial music, else unheard;
And straight I knew the Priest, from whose full heart
Welled a clear spring of quaint and sacred song,
And seemed again to tread the dewy meads
Of Sarum, and to see the thin spire pierce
The sunset skies, as I by Bemerton
Strayed rapt in thought. And as we passed, my guide:

"Not of one Church, or age, or race alone
The saints are born, nor of one clime they come,
But 'mid the grass-green English landscapes dwell!

Pure saintly souls, as by the slender towers
Of olive-grey Assisi, or white shrines
Washed by the purple sea.   There walked on earth
The saint thou seest, high of birth and name,
Yet lowly as his Lord, when once he gave
His life to Him, and with each day that dawned
Renewed his saintly vows, and lived content
For the brief years Heaven would.

                            Not always turned
His soul to Heaven; the splendours of the Court
Dazzled his youth, and the fair boundless dreams
Of youthful hope.   For he, by name and blood
A noble, 'neath our Abbey's reverend shade,
Amid the cloistered shades of Westminster,
Drank with deep draughts the lore of Greece and Rome,
And then within the time-worn Halls which watch
The slow-paced Cam; and there his studious eyes
Kept nightly vigil, and his sweet shy Muse
Tuned her clear voice for Heaven, a stainless youth

Who to his loved and gracious mother vowed
The firstlings of his song.   For him the flow
Of sweet concordant descants soothed his soul
Till Heaven stood open.   But not yet his thought
Turned to the Altar, since in high respect
And favour of his king, he stayed to take
What high advancement his unwearied thirst
For knowledge, and his gay and polished wit,
Wielding the tongues of France and Spain, and thine,
Great Dante, and his courtly presence clad
In robes of price, might offer.   Then at length,
When now his growing soul grew sick of Courts,
Yearning for Heaven, the hand of Death removed
His potent friends, and last, the king himself;
And one by one the fetters broke which bound
His soul to earth, and soon he turned to hear
His mother's pleading words; and, stronger still,
The voice within which called him set him free—
Free from himself and wholly vowed to God.

Then, when the courtiers scoffed at him and bade him
Choose him some nobler life and worthier,
Thus made he answer: 'Though the sacred name
Of priest be now despised, yet will I strive
To do it honour. All my little store
Of learning cheerful will I yield to Him
Who gave it, grieving sore I yield Him naught
Who made me His. Oh, let me strive to be
Likened to Him, and make Humility
Lovely in all men's eyes, following still
My merciful meek King.'
                              So he became
A servant of the Altar, for awhile
A deacon only, fearing yet to take
The priestly office. At the last, when now
His struggling years had reached life's midmost way,
Whence turn our faces homewards, weak in frame
Though strong in spirit, 'mid the golden meads

He ministered a priest, where the gray spire
Of Sarum points to Heaven, and consecrates
The rich low vale with grace.   There he should see
Three brief and saintly years before the end.

There from him all his courtly robes, his silks,
His sword, he put away, and in the garb
Of priesthood did endue himself, and vow
His contrite soul to Heaven.   Within his church,
With all doors closed, he passed, as the law bade,
To take full seisin, and, their pastor now,
To toll, with his own hand, the bell which called
The faithful.   Then because he came not back
After long hours, they sought him, and, behold,
Through the low casement looking, saw the saint
Prostrate before the altar, rapt in prayer
For strength to do God's work ; and there he framed
His rule of life, and vowed to keep it still.

Even so the good Priest lived his tranquil days,
His saintly helpmeet working with him still
In alms and prayer. Daily the orisons
Of those pure souls, and theirs who dwelt with them,
Three orphaned girls, rose morn and eve to Heaven,
Following the sober uses of their Church,
Matins and vespers. All the country side
Loved that white life, and knelt with reverent hearts
Whene'er within the little oratory
The daily Liturgies were sung. The hind
Paused at his task when o'er the neighbouring leas,
Summer and winter, thrilled the solemn bell
That called the saint to prayer, and oftentimes,
Touched by some new devouter impulse, left
The brooding oxen at the plough, and knelt
Awhile within the reverend walls, and took
The good man's blessing, and returned with strength
Fresh braced for toil. Thus he, within a realm

Whereon the coming shadow of strife and blood,
The fanatic's guile and hate, the atheist's sneer,
Brooded already, and the darkling stain
Of worldly ease, and sloth, and sensual sin,
Renewed the pure devotion of a Church
Stripped of its Pagan gauds and robed for Heaven.

Ah! saintly life, for which the round of praise
And duty was enough, far from the din
And noise of Courts; for which to praise the Lord
And feed His helpless poor sufficed to fill
Thy days with blessedness! I hear thee yet
Bid the poor wife who stammered forth her need
Be of good cheer, nor fear to tell thee all.
I see thee, clad in courtly silks erewhile,
Stoop when thy neighbour's wagon, with its load
Of humble produce, on the rugged way
To Sarum fell, raise him, and from the mire
Replace his burden with long toil, and then,

Giving an alms and bidding him take heed,
Even as he loved his soul, to spare his beast,
Pace half-unconscious the astonished street
Of the prim city, miry, unashamed.

But clearer yet I see thee, when the strain
Of unheard rhythms filled thy happy ears,
Wander from field to field; and on the road
To the great Minster, when thy soul had need
Of new refreshment, and upon thy way,
Hoarding faint echoes of a voice Divine,
Glow into fervent verse, and stone by stone
Build up thy 'Temple;' and anon sit rapt,
Leaving thy humbler liturgies awhile,
Within the heaven-kissed fane the centuries
Mellow, and listen to the soaring chant
Sung daily still, the jubilant anthem's voice
Of praise, the firstborn precious harmonies
Of England's sacred song; the o'ermastering joy

Of the full organ-music glooming deep
From aisle to aisle, or caught from height to height,
Till lost at last as at Heaven's gate, and thou
And thy rapt soul floated with it to joy.

Ah! blessèd blameless years, to which too soon
Stern Nature set her limit. Thy weak frame
Three little years of too great happiness
Strained first, then wore out quite; thy failing strength
First to the Minster might not bear thee more
To foretaste Heaven. Then to thy lowly church
No more thy footsteps fared. Thy oratory
Thou still didst keep; and each succeeding day,
Matins and vespers, would thy feeble voice
Give praise as thou wert wont, nor would thy soul
Deny, while still thy body could, her due
Of worship to the Lord who succoured thee,
Lauding Him always. Last, when now 'twas grown
Too weak to serve, a faithful priest and friend,

Said the loved prayers, while thou with thankful heart
Listenedst and wert content, and on thy lips
Hovered a saintly smile!

                         Now when his life
Flowed nearer to its sea, there came a priest,
Sent from his saintly friend of youth and age,
Nicholas Ferrar. 'Prithee,' cried the saint,
'Take to my friend this message. God is good,
And just in all His ways. Of His great grace
I do rejoice in that which pleaseth Him,
Ay, even to wane and die. Tell him my heart
Is fixed on Him, and waits the appointed change
With hope and patience. Sir, I pray you, give him
This little book, the portrait of long strife
Betwixt my soul and Heaven, ere yet I took
My Master's name, wherein I now go free.
See, it is called "The Temple;" it and I
Are less than His least mercies. Bid him, sir,
Burn it, if judged unhelpful to weak souls.

I prize it not. I look back from this place
On my past life, the music that I loved,
The beauty I held dear, the pleasant talk
Of books and men, and all are but a dream
And unreturning shadow, and I know
I go, as did my sires, to make my bed
In darkness; and I praise the Hand which gives
Such patience to me now, and brings me safe
Through Death's dark gate to Heaven.'
       And he, when come
To his last earthly Sunday, suddenly
Rose in his bed, and, taking in his hand
His viol, once again with feeble voice
Sang his own hymn:

  'The Sundays of Man's life,
   Threaded together on Time's string,
   Make bracelets to adorn the wife
   Of the Eternal Glorious King.

> On Sunday Heaven's gate stands ope,
> Blessings are plentiful and ripe,
> More plentiful than hope!'"

"More plentiful,"
I cried, "and poured from no unfruitful horn.
Ay, but thy hope was great, pure saint, who thus
From out thy dying chamber wentest forth
Cheerful into the void, and didst defy
The Enemy, yielding thy grateful soul
Into His hands who gave it. Shall thy life
Fade from our thoughts, dear heart? Nay, while thy clear
And yearning soul distils in verse that breathes
Fresh odours of the Heaven it loved, and decks
With quaint conceits thy Church, thy Faith, thy Lord,
As erst the kneeling kings who honoured Him
With frankincense and myrrh; nay, while the spire
Thou lovedst, still points its finger to the skies,

And this our England keeps her sober faith—
Not of the zealot born, nor of the priest—
And men still prize the gentle life and path
Of contemplation, lit with flowers of good,
And scented sweet with praise and works of ruth
And charity.   The fashion of our lives,
Our thoughts, our faiths, our Heaven may suffer change,
But this one never."

                    Next it was a man
With ruddy face and fair hair sprent with gray,
And somewhat stern of aspect, till he spoke—
A tall and vigorous form, a little bent
By too long prison years, in modest garb
A Puritan; who next in time was born
To him whom last I saw; differing in all,
In mien, in thought, in speech, yet each inspired
And saintly.   As I looked I seemed to know
The wondrous peasant, who by dreaming thought,
Fine as the Bard's who sang of Heaven and Hell,
Lightened his long duress, and for our aid
Has left a record of the Pilgrim soul

Faring to Heaven by rough and perilous ways,
Which myriads since have trod. And thus my guide:

"'Poor and of meanest rank, and most despised,'
At Elstow, in the dewy, daisied fields
Hard by the dreaming Ouse, was born the saint
Thou seest, ere yet the clang of civil strife
Frighted our land, and 'neath that large bold will
Which swayed the Commonwealth, his budding life
Ripened to manhood. In his father's home,
A humble cottage, with the timbered walls
Of older England, grew the stalwart youth
Whom blameless strength and rude untempered force
Urged sometimes headlong, prizing overmuch
The sports his skill made dear; the flying ball
Winged by the tireless arm; the joyous toil
Of emulous comrades when the deafening peal
Swung from the reeling tower, and bell with bell
Mingled reverberant chimes; the village green

When from the short sweet grass the merry din
Of youthful voices rose, till the tired sun
Lengthened the shadows, and the faint young stars
Relit the fading skies.   And oftentimes,
In his hot youthful haste, his careless tongue
Would break in reckless and impatient speech,
And oaths profane, till sober hearers shunned
The rude wild youth.   And yet his life was pure
Of grosser sin ; the Fiends of Drink and Lust
Allured him not ; only his hasty youth
Possessed his life too much, and hurried him
By earthly flower-set ways and far from Heaven.

But not the less his self-accusing soul
Suffered for his offence.   Visions by night
Oppressed his boyish sleep.   He saw Heaven's dome
Aflame with fire, the boundless firmament
Shivered by mighty thunders ; over all
The loud Archangel pealing, and a throne

Set in the East, whereon sate One whose face
Shone like the Morning Star.   Anon the earth,
Rent by a terrible earthquake, sank with him
Into the nether hell, 'mid the dread sights
And sounds of doom, when suddenly there came
One who, on shining wings descending, snatched
His fainting soul from that accursed throng;
And lo, it was a dream !
                        Soon, when the storm
Of warfare burst, upon the Midland fields,
A boy in years, against the faithless king
He served a soldier, for the cause he loved,
And saw his comrade at his side fall dead,
Shot through the brain.   Yet when that bitter strife
Was ended, to his old rude life he turned,
As reckless as of old, until he found
A sweet girl-wife, devout, whose simple faith
Loving the ancient worship drew his feet
Sunday by Sunday to the gray old church.

Matins and Vespers, and the tranquil rite,
The surpliced priest, low prayer, and soaring chant
Worked on him, and the cheerful Sunday sports,
The dance, the race, the swift unerring shaft,
When hymns and prayers were done; and so he lived
A blameless, unawakened life.
      Till last,
One fateful Sabbath morning, as he sate
Within the village church, the preacher's voice,
Bidding them keep the holy day of rest,
Seemed to the awakened conscience of the youth
To probe his inner soul. The merry throng
Crowded the green when the reproving voice
Was still, and with them he. But as his arm
Was raised to strike the ball, again the voice
Loud on his inner ear, and in the skies
A pitying Heavenly face, and all his strength
Sank nerveless, sudden as by that strange chill
Which strikes the paralytic, and he knew

Some vague awakened consciousness of guilt
And terror; but as yet no healing power
Refreshed his restless soul, only despair
And wretchlessness, and such ungoverned speech
That, hearing him, some hapless wanton once
Reproved him for his fault.
      Then with sad heart
He strove to mend. He set a ceaseless watch
Upon his careless tongue, the sports he loved
He shunned as sin, all innocent delights
He dared no more enjoy; the game, the dance,
Music at last, and song, with iron will
He put from him, and of the mellow voices
Of chiming bells and the tumultuous joy
Of mixed reverberant sound partook no more,
Standing without, beneath the reeling tower,
An outcast in the darkness, grown at last
Afraid lest haply the impending walls,
As in Siloam erst, avenged his sin.

Thus did he strive long time with his own soul,
A doubter self-accused, till one fair day,
Working in summer, in the silent streets
Of Bedford, at his task, he chanced to hear
Three humble women, sitting in the sun,
Discourse of things Divine; and all his heart
Was kindled into faith in the new birth
They spake of, and again and yet again,
Day after day, he sought them; for his soul
Cared but for Heaven alone.

       And then again,
Like his own Pilgrim, who had travelled far
From the sad City on the road to Heaven,
Yet passed to Doubting Castle, he would make
A trial of his faith, still sore afraid
Lest he had none, bidding the little pools
Of water dry because the Word had said
That whoso should believe, even as a grain

Of mustard-seed, might work all miracles;
And when he dared not put it to the touch
Fresh doubts assailed his soul.   Was he elect
Among the saints of God?   The day of Grace,
Was it not past for him?   Was there yet room
For such as he?   Ah, nay; too late! too late!
The ranks of the elect were full, the tale
Accomplished, and for him the Pit of Hell,
Naught else, for all his prayers.   'Go sin; thy fate
Is sealed, thou canst not change it,' pealed the voice
Of Evil.   But the undying voice within
Answered, 'I will not.'   And amid the gloom
Of utter hopelessness he kept his feet
From straying, though each trivial act or word
He feared might turn to ill.   Terror of death
Pressed sore on him, lest he should die in sin,
And yet he feared to live, lest haply use
Might dull that healing pain.   The lowest brute,
Nay, the poor reptile on his path, he deemed

Happier than he; or if at times he held
Some hope of heaven, the Tempter came and bade him,
In visions in the watches of the night,
Renounce the Hand which saved him. 'Sell him,' cried
The Tempter's voice within him, day and night
Sounding through every trivial act and thought,
Sleeping or waking; till one night it seemed,
After long struggles and convulsive throes,
As if at last his weary, o'erwrought brain
Assented to the wrong. And straight the day
Grew black as night, the very stones cried out
Against his sin.

    And then, oh joy! there came,
Even in the Valley of the Shadow of Death,
To this poor pilgrim soul a heavenly Light
And Voice of Comfort. All his former sins
Of doubt or word or act, he knew forgiven
Of a great Love and Grace; and happiness
Unmixed with fear, and full assurance, filled

That self-tormented soul. Rapt in high joy,
When, like St. Francis 'midst his feathered throng,
He paced the new-sown fallows whence should spring
Life's seed, as for his soul, his jubilant heart
Would almost to the cawing rooks impart
His tale of Love Divine.
     So that vexed soul
Found peace at last, and saw with clearer sight
"The heights of grace and love and mercy." Soon
Within the lustral waters of the Ouse
His life was cleansed, and thenceforth dedicate
To preach the Word he loved, his eloquent speech,
Not tongue-tied by the learning of the schools,
Speaking to sinners. As one from the dead,
As one who bore a fire, oppressed by guilt
And terror, came he, whom nor guilt nor hell
Could silence, but 'neath humble roofs and low,
Or on the village green, beneath the skies,
Always he preached the Word. The liturgies

Dear to the saintly Herbert drew him not,
For whom each prayer rose new-born from the heart
To clothe itself in words, and so he spake
With full assurance, soul to soul, and led,
In part despite his creed, men's careless lives
To good and was content. Ay, though the fire
Of fierce sectarian passion and loud strifes
Swept the enfranchised land, and slander's tooth
Assailed his peace, yet worked he for his Lord
And was content.

     But on those halcyon days
Broke the intolerant law. The warning came
That he, on pain of weary prisoned years,
And exile, and the bondsman's death in life,
Should preach the Word no more. He took no heed,
But when they closed his place of praise and prayer,
In sheds or barns, or 'mid the shadowy woods,
He spake to kindling souls. Last, when the law
Forbade the freedom more, he scorned to obey,

Since if it were a sin to meet, and draw
All men to follow Christ, then sin he would.

Therefore to prison haled they him, away
From his loved home.   His dear and ailing wife
He left ; his helpless children four he left ;
And one, his little daughter blind from birth,
Whom more than life he loved, to the hard world
And penury and suffering years he left,
To do God's will; though all his father's heart
Yearned to them, knowing all the bitter pains,
Cold, hunger, nakedness, which should await
The lives his faith made orphan.   Yet his heart
Was steadfast.   'I must do His will, I must,
And venture all for Him.'
       And so his feet,
Pacing this weary wilderness, at length
Came on a certain place where was a Den,
And there he laid him down for twelve long years,

And dreamt his deathless dream.

                                        Dear prison cell
Above all others blest! where self-immured,
Because he might not purchase liberty
With silence from good words, that suffering soul
Languished long years, no cloistered convent pure
Bore rarer fruit than thine, nor hermitage
Beneath the desert stars. There lives no race
Of Christian men but dreams thy dream, nor creed
But holds it dear, because its clear voice calls
Deep in the sacred silence of the soul!

For here it was that Christian rose and fled
The City of Destruction, and alone
Toiled on the rugged, narrow way, to where
The wicket gate was set, and a fair light
To guide to it. Here fell his feet awhile
Into the Slough of Despond. Here he found
The House of the Interpreter, and climbed

The Hill of Difficulty, and reposed
Within the Palace Beautiful, and slept
In Peace, and from the ramparts with the dawn
Looked down upon Emmanuel's land, a fair
And smiling country, rich with flowers and fruits
And water-springs, and on the further heaven
Flushed with the rising Sun, the untrodden snows
Of the Delectable, Eternal Hills,
Hard by the City of God. And here he took
His armour, and went fearless down to fight
Apollyon, and prevailed, and saw beneath,
Stretched in thick darkness, filled with dreadful sounds,
The Valley of the Shadow of Death, and dared
To thread the darkling pass, where piteous wails,
And rising fiery smoke, and dead men's bones,
And dreadfuller, the onward rushing flight
Of Fiends unseen, the spectral shades of Doubt,
Assailed his steadfast soul. And here he saw
Vanity Fair, the sad world's counterfeit,

Wherefrom the martyred Pilgrim passed to Heaven.
And here the dungeon glooms of Doubting yawned
The stronghold of Despair, which held him fast
Whose lips had tasted of the River of Life.
Here smiled the plains of Beulah, and beyond
Stole the dark deep which all mankind must cross,
Sinner and saint; and here the golden domes
Of the Celestial City beamed on him
Who after Life's sad pilgrimage was blest!

But when to his dear home he came again,
After twelve years of prison, free to preach
His message as he would, he knew what change
Time brings to all; dead was his sightless girl,
And bare his humble home. So with brave heart
He set himself to work, but chiefly vowed
His toil to Heaven. To labour for his Church
Was all his joy, and yet his worldly store
Increased, and he in great respect of men,

With his good wife, among his stalwart boys,
Flourished long busy years; and all the doubt
And misery of old were gone, and clear
The sunset of the evening of his days
Shone on him, tranquil gold.   Through all the strife
Of those dark troubled times, he lived unmoved
A peaceful life, scorning the narrow bonds
Dear to the zealot, broad in tolerance
For every Christian creed or rite or name
Which loved the Spirit of God; and toiled for souls
In his dear native town, and was content.

Then while as yet his green, unbroken age
Was vigorous, came the end which comes at last
To all things living.   One there was whose wrath
Burned fierce against his son, and he who knew
The blessing of the Peacemakers was fain
To reconcile the pair.   And as he rode
Loving his task, upon the wintry way

A sudden rain-storm chilled his weary frame,
And fever racked his limbs. Ten suffering days
He lingered far from home, and with the cry,
' Take me—to Thee I come,' breathed out his life."

Which things when I had heard, my kindling soul
Burst into words : " Oh, precious gift and rare
Of Heaven, which from the slough of common life,
And stony wastes of penury, despite,
Oppression, want, despondency, canst raise
The perfumed rose of Fancy, and the pure
White lily of the Saint ! Ah, not alone
In cloistered convents cold, or storied shrines,
Springs up the saintly life, nor in the Halls
Of Learning blooms the flawless flower of thought !
Myriads of faltering feet have trod the road
Thou troddest once, and fought and fallen, or come
Through thee to victory, and as they pass,

Fired with a broader faith and wider hope
Than that thou knewest; on their painful way,
Not wholly thine, but to the self-same goal,
Still solaced by thy precious allegory,
Take thee and thy quaint Dream for staff and guide,
Throughout the perilous pilgrimage to Heaven."

Then came another, of priestly garb and mien,
A young man still, wanting the years of Christ,
But long since with the saints.   Not as the priest
Of Sarum, or that peasant pilgrim, he
A poet with the contemplative gaze
And listening ear, but quick of force and eye,
Who fought the wrong without, the wrong within,
And, being a pure saint, like those of old,
Abased himself and all the precious gifts
God gave him, flinging all before the feet
Of Him whose name he bore—a fragile form
Upon whose hectic cheek there burned a flush
That was not health; who lived as Xavier lived,
And died like him upon the burning sands,
Untended, yet whose creed was far from his

As pole from pole; whom grateful England still
Loves, though his face I knew not.   And my guide,
Breathing his name, spake thus:

        "In Truro town,
Hard by the wave-worn headlands of the West,
When now the eighteenth century of the Faith
Drew near its end, its martyr that should be
Was Henry Martyn born.   His father's arm
Long in the dark abysses of the mine
Slaved for his children's bread.   His little son,
A weakly boy and studious, sate apart,
Shunning the school's rude games, too oft the sport
Of coarser wills and stronger, till he found
A stout young arm, upon whose ready aid
He rested and was happy; and his keen
And vivid brain grew stronger, and his thirst
For knowledge, till at length, a boy in age,
To Granta's venerable halls he went,

A student not obscure, and with hard toil
Laboured four happy years of blameless youth,
And took at last the foremost place, and rose
To fame and honour of men, and reaped the high
Reward of studious hours, the untroubled life
Spent in the contemplative courts where comes
No murmur of the world, but only thought
And knowledge draw the thinker, till sometimes
The careless soul, missing the wholesome stir
Of daily care, grows slothful, the quick brain
Sinks low in indolent ease and base content,
And bears no worthy fruit.
      But not for him
These perils were, because a higher thirst—
Higher than wealth, or ease, or honour of men,
Or learning's self—possessed his yearning soul;
When the same friend who helped his friendless youth,
Now to a full and finer manhood grown,
Bade him do all things not for fame of men,

But for God's glory. And his sister's voice
Thrilled on him in the pure unworldly words
Of simple fervour. Not at first his soul
Gave heed, impatient with those warning words,
And fired with youthful pride and hot pursuit
Of flying knowledge; but at length the spark
Kindled within him, and the sudden loss
Of the dear father of his love laid bare
The chambers of his soul, and filled his heart
With other thoughts than earth's, till, when he gained
The meed of all his hopes, which opened to him
The path of earthly honour, the youth's heart
Knew, with a sick surprise, his empty hand
Grasped but a shadow.

     Then the awakened gaze,
Turned wholly from the earth; on things of Heaven
He dwelt both day and night. The thought of God
Filled him with infinite joy; his craving soul
Dwelt on Him as a feast, as did the soul

Of rapt Francesco in his holy cell
In blest Assisi; and he knew the pain,
The deep despondence of the saint, the doubt,
The consciousness of dark offence, the joy
Of full assurance last, when Heaven itself
Stands open to the ecstasy of faith.

Therefore, though all men smiled on him, though smooth
Life's path lay stretched before him—wealth and fame,
The dignity of learning, the high meed
Which crowns the pleader's skill, the Senate itself,
Waiting his keen young brain—he turned from all
To that untried, laborious way which lay
Across wide seas, to spend a lonely life
Spreading the light he loved, beneath the glare
Of tropic skies, by desert sands and wilds
Far from all Christian converse, and the gain
Of our long eighteen centuries, and pine
Alone 'mid millions, knowing not his Lord;

The Brahmins' fables, the relentless lie
Of Islam—these he chose to bear, who knew
How swift the night should fall on him, and burned
To save one soul alive while yet 'twas day.
This filled his thoughts, this only, and for this
On the pure altar of his soul he heaped
A costlier sacrifice, this youth in years,
For whom Love called, and loving hands, and hope
Of childish lives around him, offering these,
Like all the rest, to God.
      Yet when his hour
Was come to leave his England, was it strange
His weakling life pined for the parting kiss
Of love and kindred, whom his prescient soul
Knew he should see no more, and, week by week
Tossed on the wandering wave, driven back once more
By battling winds, looked with deep longing eyes
On the dear shore? Yet never did he pray
The cup might pass from him, not when the curse

Of war assailed his gentle eyes and wrung
His soul with agony.   A priest, he filled
All priestly duty, though his shuddering soul
Shrank from the sight of blood.   Through storm and stress
And perils of the sea, through all despite
Of scoffing men, who lent no willing ear
To his high message, still the humble saint
Was instant in his work, and bore the jeers
And unbelief around him, he who left
His place of honour for the Faith, and did
His uncomplaining service.   Thus at last
He reached the Indian shore, where he would spend
His life in saintly labours till the end.

There ten long years he toiled on, day by day,
Writing his patient record of a soul
Which struggles for the Right.   The home of friends
Who cared for him and Heaven, and would have kept
    him,

Impatient for his work, he left behind,
And straight, across the burning plains, alone,
Sped, cheerful, where no ray of Christ had risen
To break the age-long gloom; there, solitary,
Unfriended, solaced by no answering soul,
With little blessing on his work, or fruit
Of his great toil, reproaching every hour
He lost for God, knowing how short his span,
And how immense his task, now preaching oft
To careless ears, now spending his keen brain
As when he wrought for fame and honour of men,
With Munshi and with Pundit, if his skill
Might give to each, in his own tongue, the Word,
He spent his youth. Last, when his task of love
Was done, and seven long years of ceaseless toil
Had worked their will on him, there came fresh griefs
To try his faith. The woman of his love
Feared to leave all and give her life to his,
And both to God; his sisters passed away

To Heaven, nor saw him more. There seemed on earth
Nothing for which to live, except the Faith ;
The last of all his race, unloved, alone—
Only the Faith, the Faith ! until his soul
Wore thin her prison bars, and he was fain
To rest awhile, or work no more the work
For which alone he lived.
                         Then over seas
Once more he took his way, leaving the land
Where he had hoped to die, along the roll
Of the warm tropic wave. Once more he saw
Ceylon's green palm-fringed shore, the sumptuous tomb
Of him, his brother of old, who strove like him
To spread the Faith, and, like him, died for it,
S. Francis Xavier, and among the caves
Of storied Elephanta stayed ; but soon,
His great zeal firing him, took ship again,
And, after weary wanderings, gained at last
The Persian wastes, and took the difficult way

To Shiraz through the desert.   Day by day
The fierce sun blazed upon the sands; by night
The dead air, like a furnace blast, assailed
His fevered frame, and parched him and consumed him
With horrible thirst, and robbed his eyes of sleep
Till life was well-nigh spent.   And then the hand
Which seemed to guide him always led his feet
To a sweet vale, England in sight and sound,
Hidden in the horrible waste, where cool airs blew,
Streams ran, and birds sang clear, and wheat was gold.
Then all his faithful heart burst forth in praise,
As did the Kingly Bard's : ' He maketh us
To lie down in green pastures, and beside
The clear cool waters leadeth.'   Thus his soul
Made laud, and was content, praising the Lord,
In Shiraz.
            There one happy toilsome year
He sojourned.   Day by day the sages came
Who held the faith of Islam, and would hear

Of Him whose Name he taught. Through the long days
He laboured at his work, spending the gifts
God lent him, for the Faith. Last, when at length
The Gospel spake to Persian ears, he bore
His work to Tabriz, where he sought the King,
Faring by night along the moonlit vales,
Through bowery lanes, where the loud nightingales
Thrilled the white fields with song. Then feverish heats
Burned him upon his way, and sapped his strength;
And when, weak unto death, he reached the place
Where the King sojourned late, he found him not,
Only his courtiers' scorn. Then his great heart
Broke in impatient words. 'My God,' he cried,
'What have I done that men should mock me thus,
Save only love for Thee?' And when he turned
Despairing homeward, soon again he pined
Prostrate in pain, the fever seizing him
Two weary months, and his brain burned like fire,
A present death in life. Yet not the less

His faithful soul bare witness to the Faith.
Rejection, sickness, torment—what are these
To the believer's thought! And when he rose,
Musing upon the enormous waste which lay
'Twixt him and home, whither, his brave work done,
His longing eyes were turned, his weary heart
Fainted within him, and he looked no more
To press the hands he loved. Hopeless he fared
On his last journey. 'Neath the fabled peak
Of Ararat he stayed awhile, to rest
In the hushed convent with the Armenian monks,
A cheerful guest. And then again the grip
Of fever clutched him, and depressed his soul
With sad forebodings. Yet he struggled still
Towards Stamboul, though the plague slew day by day
Its thousands, and the affrighted tribes around
Fled the advancing Death. 'Thy will be done;
Living or dying, oh, remember me!'
Thus writes the dying saint. And then long days

Of misery, which his languid hand records,
When now a fire consumed him, now the cold
Of palsy left him ice.   Laid on the ground,
His soul was filled with God, his Company,
His Friend, his Comforter.   'Oh, when shall Time
Be done, and that new Heaven and Earth appear
Where dwelleth Righteousness?'   Thus his hand traced
Its last pure words.   Then but a few brief hours,
And he unfriended, far from help and home,
Alone, but having Christ, with no kind hand
To close the eyes which saw the joys unseen
And vision of the blest, worn out, in pain—
Whether of fever or the deadly force
Of pestilence, none knoweth—breathed his last,
And bore the martyr's palm."

                               And then once more
I seemed to hear a voice,—was it my guide,

Or my own soul?—discourse:

      "Shall any ask,
Was all thy suffering naught, because the strength
Of Error still bears sway? Ah! too brief life,
So jealous of each hour, and counting lost
Each day not vowed to Heaven. What, hadst thou known
Thy labour thus in vain? Fourscore long years
Have passed since thou, like kindred souls to-day,
Diedst for the Truth; the long, slow, barren years
Mock us and all our toil. Hadst thou done well
To reap a little while thy well-earned meed
Of Thought in lettered ease? Hadst thou done well
To give thee to the pleader's art, and strive
To make the Wrong seem Right, and sink at last
To wealth and praise of men, seeking, a judge
Scorning the graceless sophistries of old,
To cure thy former ill—thou whose keen brain
Had doubtless borne thee far? Hadst thou done well
To doze slow hours, sunk deep in mitred ease,

Soothed by sweet chants, lost in the vaporous grey;
Or, a great preacher, mark the moistened eyes,
Flushed cheeks, and quick-drawn breaths thy facile tongue
Had stirred, thyself unmoved; or shine a light
Of the Senate, till thy peers in high debate
Bowed to thy eloquent speech, and thou shouldst guide
The helm of our great England? Was it well
To hold this strange Twin-Nature of our Race,
Which soars so high and sinks so low, as thou.
Unutterably vile in thought, in will,
In every action vile, trampling thy soul
In dust before thy God, who made thee too,
And all things, and has left us free to take
The path we would, to Heaven or hell, and knows
His work not wholly base, nor framed too fine
For this our place of trial? Nay, I know
How many ways of safety He displays
To the awakened soul—the way thou trodd'st,
The way of San Francesco's blessèd cell,

The honourable trivial road which leads
By silent saintly liturgies of home
Up to the selfsame Heaven. But this I know
Is certain, that thy lifelong sacrifice
Was best for thee, and best the voice which called
From love and friendship, ay, from all good things
Which make life happy, to the burning plains
Where thou shouldst spend thy few and evil days
Of toil and suffering, pouring forth thy life
Like water for the Faith, shedding thy blood
As did of old the Martyrs, drop by drop,
Upon the ungrateful sand of heathen hearts."

And then I saw a stately figure come,
Which seemed to wear the quaint and dovelike robe
Of silver-grey, the lawn that hid the hair,
The modest decent garb they love who vow
Their lives to Heaven, albeit no cloistered bars
Withdraw them from the world, but build around
A nunnery, and, 'mid the noise and din
Of all the sensual and wrongful world,
An oratory where the Spirit may dwell
And, long-awaited, claim its own; the band
Who struck the fetters from the slave, who tend
The halt and sick, and spend themselves in works
Of mercy for the prisoners who lie bound
In chains their sins have forged; and straight my eyes

Knew whom it was they saw, before my guide,
With grave voice softening as it went, replied
To my unspoken thought.

      "A hundred years
Have passed since she thou seest, on the earth
Came first, of gentle birth and wealth and ease,
Where the grey Anglian city in the east
Broods round its central spire. A blooming girl,
In her gay youth she trod with eager feet
The path of innocent pleasure; none more blithe
At chase or festal than the lithe young form
Who in her scarlet habit loved to fly
Across the rushing fields, or listen rapt
To stirring martial melodies, or tread
The giddy measures of the dance, and take,
With her young motherless sisters, what delight
Beseemed their youth. Then, in her budding age,
When only seventeen summers smiled on her,

The joys she scarce had known began to pall,
And she reproached herself with every thought
Which stole her hours from Heaven.   Blind dreams of
    good,
Yearnings for something higher than she knew,
Took her, and, knowing this perplexèd world
Moves towards the best, she felt her drifting life
A hapless bark which fronts the gathering storm
Without a pilot's skill.   But the great Hand
Was with her not the less, though yet unseen,
And soon the pleading of a kindred soul
Sent over seas woke in her inmost depths
Assurance mixt with tears, and presently
The dull world faded from her, and she gave
Her all to Heaven.   Then all her costly robes
She left, and took the habit of a Friend
And their plain speech—slowly, and half ashamed,
Lest those who knew her scoffed ; but not the less
She was convinced, and held the Faith to the end.

Thence through her long sweet life, her own hand writes
Her daily story. Through what deeps of doubt
And self-distrust, high yearnings, often dashed
By that o'erwhelming sense of grave offence
Which takes the saints alone, and oftentimes
What high and glorious certitudes of faith,
The heavens standing open, and the Lord
With gracious beckoning hand, they know who read
The story of her days. Love came to her,
And happy wedlock, and unclouded years,
And fair-grown offspring. All good things to hold,
Honour and high obedience, troops of friends,
A heart which turned to Heaven and dwelt with God—
All these were hers. Ofttimes she spake the Word,
Spurning the conscious weakness of her sex
And her own shrinking modesty; ofttimes
She nursed the sick, and did relieve with alms
The needy, works of mercy and of faith

Filling her life. And yet, not all-content
With such high duty, still her yearning soul,
Which not the weight of daily household care,
Nor love of spouse or children, satisfied,
Panted for more, and hastened to the work
Which keeps her memory green, and crowns her Saint,
And raised her to the skies.

      'Twas in the foul
And crowded prison wards her pitying heart
Found its own work. Three hundred hapless lives
Huddled together, starving, naked, vile—
The innocent and guilty, the poor soul
Who stepped a foot-pace from the path of good,
Mewed side by side within that narrow jail
With those who had put off, for desperate years,
The last thin rags of shame; a dreadful band,
Brutal, unclean, without a bed to rest
Their miserable limbs, save the damp floor
Of the foul, reeking dungeon. Frenzied cries

Of rank offence, blaspheming God and man,
Worse than of madness, smote the shrinking ear;
And 'mid the dreadful throng, more piteous still,
The teeming ranks of children, the shrill note
Of childish voices trained in all the lore
Of wickedness, to beg, to sot, to steal,
To curse. Each sight and sound that had made Hell
More dreadful than before, the sight of lives
Which had been innocent once, now doomed and damned,
Forlorn of men, and quite forgot by God!

Nay, not forgotten! Since one human heart
Felt pity for them still. The faithful soul
Of that good nursing-mother blazed afire,
Hearing and seeing, and her inmost depths
Were kindled into flame. But not at once
Might she begin her life-work. Birth and Death,
Young lives that came and went, the loss of friends
And brethren, that strange hush and chill which comes

To every home when first the young flock dares
To spread weak wings and tempt the perilous air
Far from the nest—these held her three long years
Far from the work she loved.

                            And then one day
She found her footsteps free, and took her way
To the grim prison where that hapless crowd
Rotted in sin.   Alone, with none to aid,
Like the old seer among the ravening jaws,
Or that diviner Figure which beamed hope
To the poor prisoned spirits waiting long
The Beatific End, she passed and brought
The light of fuller Day, with mild eyes filled
With gentle pity for their sin, with voice
So clear, so soft, so musical, the tongue
As of an angel.   'Mid the noise, the din
Of blasphemy, and rank offence, she spake
And hushed all other sound, except the noise
Of weeping from repentant hearts, and told

How, even at the eleventh hour, the Lord
Was strong to save, telling of Him she served,
Whose name they knew not yet; and on the depths
Of those poor rayless souls, sunk deep in ill,
Shone with some pure reflected light of Heaven,
And touched—a mother herself—the mothers' hearts
With pity for the children who should come
To ill as they did, till the spark Divine,
Which never dies out quite, shone out once more,
And once again, from out the sloughs of sin,
Uprose toward Heaven some faint fair flower of good.

Thus she, and with her a devoted band
Of women, strove for God. With instant prayer
She pleaded with them; clothing, shelter, food
She gained for them, and tidings of the Word.
And for those hapless childish lives she found
Fit teaching; those poor souls the pitiless law
Doomed to the felon's end, she fortified,

As did of old S. Catharine, with her prayers
Even at the gate of Death.

                        Nor could her pity
Stay here, nor bear the intolerable load
Of the uncaring law which played with life
As might a tiger, stern, exacting blood
For every trivial ill. With those vile powers
Unfaith and selfishness, which ruled the world
And mar it yet and will, she strove with might,
And did at last prevail; and ere she died,
No more the shameless wickedness was done
Which from all time had shed the innocent blood
In the pure name of Law, staking a life
Against each venial wrong. Oh, clear-eyed soul,
That saw the Right undimmed, above the mists
That blinded worldly eyes, because it knew
The rule of Right, one with the Law of God!

But not alone her works of mercy touched

The prisoner in his cell. When to their doom
Of slavery, worse than death, the senseless law
Had sent those hapless lives, over wide seas,
To the far underworld, it prisoned them
Mixed as of yore, the felon old in sin,
The almost innocent, and the young lives
Of children mewed together, month on month
Festering between the crowded decks, till came
The day when they were flung upon the shore
Of a new land, helpless, unclothed, unfed,
Tainted by forced companionship with ill,
To die of want or only live by sin.
These wrongs her prescient eye foresaw and gave
Her thought to mend. The young lives new to wrong
She from the guiltier set apart, and all,
When the new world loomed on their wondering gaze,
Found hands of welcome. Oft, in some frail skiff
Daring the wintry Thames, ere the sad ship
Sailed with its load, her soft imploring voice

Rose high for all, commending them to Heaven,
And pleading with such gentle words and pure,
Their hard hearts melted, and the flowing tears
Relieved their pain ; and on the deck around
The rude rough seamen heard, without a word,
The saint's high message and the sweet clear tones,
And grew ashamed to scoff, while as she knelt
The helpless women checked their gathering tears,
In silence till the dark boat on the stream
Was lost in night, and took their only friend.

Thus throughout all the land, year after year,
She cleansed each teeming prison. The chill North
She traversed, and the melancholy West,
And by the perilous seas which welter round
The still-vexed Channel Isles, thence to fair France,
Still seeking what of help she could for those
Whom their sin prisoned fast, and the low plains
Of deep-sunk Holland. Where her footsteps turned

She left a blessing. From the Russian snows
Came news of those her high example drew
To kindred deeds of mercy. Courts and Thrones
Paid fitting honour to her work, and she,
Amid the felons now, now set on high
With Queens to do her honour, kept unchanged
Her humble heart, breathing the self-same prayer:
'By any ways, by any paths Thou wilt,
So men may come to knowledge of Thy Truth.'

But not the less the changing, chanceful world
Pressed on her, than on those blest souls of old.
The wealth she only prized because it gave
Power to do good; which gathers day by day
To crush the miser with its load, from her
Was taken for no fault; her stately home
She left a blameless exile. Time and Death
Knocked loudly at her doors. The saintly band,
Brothers and sisters, thinned; the loving eyes

Of children closed untimely; the young lives
Of children's children went, leaving her age
To mourn them.   Fever coming swept the home
Of her dear son, and took him, the strong stay
Of his young flock.   Who reads her story knows
A gathering tale of loss, to which each year
Brought its own added sum.   Her natural force,
Before the allotted span, grew faint and weak,
And, spent with pain, month after month she lay
In suffering, till she prayed, if 'twere God's will,
That she might be at rest; and sometimes, weak
And sore beset, her saintly humbleness
Was dashed with self-distrust, and she who felt
The Everlasting Arms beneath her, knew
The natural fear which ofttimes vexes less
The sinner than the saint.
                          So when her hour
Was come, her children round her, she prepared
To meet the Lord she loved.   She whose long life

Was lived for Him; whose earliest waking thought
Was every morn for Him; whose gathering years
Were crowned with deeds of mercy; whose dear name,
In every clime, thousands of rescued souls
Uttered with tremulous lips and full of praise;
Whose thought was always how to raise to hope
The poor, the sick, the fallen; how to strike
The fetters from the prisoner and the slave;
And save the piteous childish lives the State
Had left to certain ruin—she no less
Knew the Divine despondency which marks
The saintly soul. 'Pray for me,' said her voice;
'It is a strife, but I am safe.'"

"Dear saint,
Ay, thou wert safe," I cried, "because thy heart
Was humble! To what heights of purity,
What inaccessible awful precipices
Of duty, didst thou turn thy gaze whose soul

Knew this diviner failure? To what depths
Of inner heaven, to what perfectness
Of Him thy Great Exemplar, didst thou strain?
Not only in the cloister the rapt soul
Dwells with Him, or beneath the midnight stars
Mingles with Him and bears the sacred wounds
Of the Passion, but along the well-trod road
Of daily trivial life the race is run
To where the crown awaits them, and the palm.
Who loves the Right, loves Him who taught it too ;
And whoso loves his brother, loves his Lord."

And then there came, last risen to the skies,
The newest of the saints I marked, who went
Only one brief year since to bear the palm
And wear the crown, a priest whose comely youth,
Dark kindly eyes, and broad and thoughtful brow
Showed still to haunting fancy marks of care,
Sobering its new-found joy. The gentle gaze
Lighted the gracious face, no longer scarred
By fell disease, that was his cross, his crown ;
And with a double tenderness my guide
Made answer softly to my silent quest.

" From the long wave of the Pacific Sea
Rise the enchanted islands of the West.

There the green surge, translucent, flowered with foam,
Breaks creaming on the strand beneath the palms;
But from its tepid waters came no sound
Of rippling mirth, nor more the fair brown forms,
Half heathen, naked, joyous, crowned with flowers,
Floated as erst on the caressing wave,
Because some strange immedicable hurt
Consumed them, and they pined in hopeless pain,
Despairing, till a servant of the Lord
Was sent to them with succour for their need,
And cleansed the desperate lives, which, struck by doom,
Cursing their fate, turned them to reckless ill;
And gave his life to serve them, till he died,
A leper in their midst.
     At Tremeloo,
Upon the far-off Belgian plain, was born
He whom the admiring tongues of half the world
Call Damien. All the story of his days

Is full of pureness. A strange child, engrossed
In musing thought, he with the shepherds loved
To drive afield ere now the opening morn,
Loosed from its flood-gates in the illumined east,
O'erflowed the slumbering plains. There all day long,
A lamb amid the innocent lambs, in play
He whiled away the hours, till all his kin
And kindly neighbours knew his childish name,
' The Little Shepherd ; ' and the lessons learnt
From solitary musings, with the broad
Still plain around, and the unbounded vault
Of Heaven above him, and no sound of life
Save bleating flocks and humming bees and songs
Of mounting larks, inspired his brooding thought
With visions not of earth, and framed his lips
To an unspoken praise ; and when he heard
The ' Angelus ' thrill o'er the twilight fields,
His childish soul rejoiced, and his young knees
Were bent in prayer, till all the country side

Cherished the strange grave child.

                                      And once, men tell,
At Whitsuntide, the holy feast, there was
A neighbouring fair of simple revelry,
And since the dawn none saw him. When they searched
The crowded village streets, they found no trace
Of the young truant; but his grandsire went,
Knowing his faith, to seek him, and, indeed,
He was not 'mid the careless peasent throng,
Nor jovial haunts of rustic merriment,
But in the church; for in the darkling aisles
They found the young child kneeling, rapt, alone,
Breathing some simple prayer. For all his soul
Was full of the Unseen, and all his heart
Turned heavenward as the sunflower to the sun.

But when his childish days were past, and now
Youth blossomed in him, youth with dim grave thoughts
And scarce confessed designs, he would not take

Thought of the priestly office yet, but spent
His ardent, eager life in wholesome cares
Fitting his budding age.   Yet was his soul
Maiden and pure, and all who knew the boy
Praised his white life.   Till one day, when his years
Touched close on manhood, in a church he knelt,
Where some strong Preacher, fired with faith in good,
Spake burning words; and straight his ardent heart
Kindled, and all night long he knelt and prayed
For guidance, and Heaven came to him and rapt
That yearning soul, so that he would no more
Do his own work, but God's.

       And so he took
The priestly office, and there came command—
The priest, his brother, lying like to die—
He in his stead should bear the lamp of Faith
To the far isles of the Pacific Sea,
Across the world, alone.   And when he heard,
His glad heart leapt within him, for he knew

That thus he best should do God's will and work
His work upon the earth.
                      After long months
Of storm tost days and perilous, with the spring,
Upon the day of his good patron saint,
S. Joseph, to his fated shore he came,
Hawaii, where he laboured year by year
In happiness, doing his Master's work
With ceaseless toil. Once on a mountain side
He paused, knowing that somewhere nigh lay hid
A Christian village, where the hungry souls
Waited their coming priest. When, with great toil
Of hand and foot, on the precipitous steep
Climbing, he gained the summit, lo! beneath
A cavernous chasm yawned; but nowhere saw he
Traces of men. Yet, without thought of doubt,
He, by new difficult crags ascending, spied
Another loftier hill, and climbed again
And reached the summit; but again no trace

Of men or dwellings, but a lonely plain,
And then again a hill; and so at last,
After long toil, spent, bleeding hand and foot,
Calling to mind the sufferings on the Tree,
And that for those poor souls his Master died,
Tottering he found his people, and confirmed
Their faith, and was rewarded for his toil.

But while his long laborious days he spent
In service of his Lord, his pitying eyes
Took many a sight of grievous misery
Which nought might heal.   For on those blessèd isles,
Where sea and sky wear a perpetual smile,
And all the lavish earth with flower and fruit
Laughs always, and from out the odorous gloom
Of blossomed trees a myriad creepers hang
Laden with perfume, and the feathery fronds
Of giant ferns spring upward twice the height
Of a man's stature, and bright birds flash by

On jewelled wings, a thousand brilliant hues,
Flower-like, among the flowers, and the clear sea
Holds in its azure deeps a thousand lights
Of sapphire scales, or gold, or glowing red,
Or tints which match the rainbow's all in one,
Brighter than any which the cunning skill
Of painter limns; and, 'midst the tropic wealth
Of lustrous blossoms strange to Northern eyes,
Sweet roses blush, and lilies veined with gold
Droop their fair heads, and starry myrtles wake
Memories of classic grace;—amidst all these
And the poor joyous lives which, crowned with flowers,
Like the old careless gods of Pagan eld,
Let the hours pass, and were content, nor knew
Our Northern cares, nor thought of hell or Heaven,
Nought but delight; there came long years ago,
Brought from the teeming East, a dreadful ill,
Which nought might cure, and seized those hapless limbs,
And rotted them away, mere death in life,

Maimed horribly, and losing human form
And semblance, till at last the wretched spirit
Released itself and fled.   And since the touch
Of hand or robe was thought to take with it
The dread contagion, from the land they chased
Those hapless sufferers, to where there rose
Sheer from the Southern Sea the frowning cliffs
Of Molokai.   On its northern edge
The island rises into purple peaks,
With soaring heads veiled in a fleece of white,
And down each steep precipitous gorge the gleam
Of leaping waters issuing from the clouds
Lights the dark cliffs, and, where a sunbeam strikes,
Sparkles in rainbow mists; and at the foot
Of those great walls, just raised above the surge,
Stretches an emerald plain, white with the homes
Of lepers, none beside.   Thither, when now
The unerring symptoms of that dreadful ill
Had shown in them, the hapless exiles sailed,

Bidding a last farewell to home and kin,
And love and life, till the slow-working plague
Consumed their limbs away.   No hope was theirs,
Nor fear of God or man ; only their doom,
Fixed on them undeserving, filled their souls
With horror and despair, and careless hate
Of Heaven, and utter recklessness of ill,
Since doomed they were, and an unchecked desire
To enjoy, since die they must.   And so it came
That these poor lives, pining in misery,
Blasphemed their fate and lived in present hell.
Yet, since no more they might return, nor those
Who tended them, long time they pined with none
To care for them, till one day, when the ship
Sailed with its fatal load, and the saint took
His last farewells with tears, the fire of Faith
Flamed up within his heart.   Without a word
To friends, or care for clothing or for food,
Of a sudden Damien leapt on board, and went

Joyful to meet his doom of pain and death,
Like the brave saints of old ; and for our age,
Our weakling age, sick of a deadly doubt,
Renewed the primal ecstasy of Faith !

There, sixteen years among those hapless folk,
He laboured. Long, beneath no sheltering roof
But open to the winds and rains of heaven
He slept, when sleep he might ; for all his hours
Were spent to bring to God the perishing souls
Their great despair corrupted. Everywhere
His cheerful smile and faithful words allured
The lives his hands relieved, and everywhere
The people, struggling back to love and right,
Left the old vices of despair, the drink
That brought oblivion, and the sensual depths
Wherein they wallowed late, devoid of hope,
Forlorn of God ; and day by day the sound
Of prayer and praise arose where blasphemies

Had rent the shuddering air.   And since the power
Of lustral waters oftentimes works out
A miracle upon the tainted soul
As on the body, and what cleanses this
Makes pure the other; from a clear cold pool
High on the mountain, fed by rain and cloud,
He led the full stream's salutary flow
To every hut where lay those hopeless lives;
And straight those wretched lairs grew clean, the plague
Lightened, and with it pain, and their lips blessed
The saint who succoured them, and, through him, God,
And sinned no more, and hope reviving wrought
Its precious spell, and happy flower-set homes
Rose where the lepers huddled ere he came,
Rotting in misery, and the pious care
Of brethren far away, learning his need,
Sent food and money for his aid, and all
Was of his hand.   And eager helpers came,
Nor of his Church alone, though of his Lord—

Brothers and sisters brave, who work to-day
His blessèd work, though he is dead and gone.

Likewise he built a hospice, where the sick
Were gently tended. There, through every day,
He laboured in their midst, spake words of hope,
Dressed their sad wounds, brought them what delicate
    food
His means supplied, and when they came to die
Paid the last rites, and with his own hands laid
The dead in earth ; and when the plague had rapt
Their hapless parents, 'twas his fostering hand
Cared for the orphans, doomed, maybe, to die
The same dread death, and pine meanwhile in pain.
And as faith's tide rose higher in their souls
He, with his own hands, planned and built a shrine
For long processions, and the solemn Mass
Served upon purest gold. So the swift days
Passed, and amid the misery around,

As one who bore a charmèd life, the saint
Laboured unscathed for twelve long toilsome years,
A father to the orphan, to the sick
A kind physician, to the suffering soul
A priest in every strait, and, when the end
Was come, a reverent hand to close the eyes
And smooth the maimèd limbs, and lay in earth
The poor dead clay whose life was hid with God.

Thus toiled he long contented years; and then
The creeping numbness took him, and he knew,
Though with no bodily sign as yet, nor scar,
Nor strength diminished, that the common doom
Waited him too. He did not quail, nor pine
That those long happy, useful years had reached
Their sure approaching term—the hand of God
Was over all, health, sickness, life and death—
' Fiat voluntas tua ; ' and he toiled
With scarce diminished strength, and zeal which knew

No shadow of abatement, through long years,
A leper like the rest. And when he preached,
And when he toiled among the sick, or gave
His Church's solemn office, all his words
Were of 'us lepers,' glorying in the load
The will of Heaven assigned to him, and proud,
Even as his dear Lord touched with healing hand
The lepers of old time and made them whole,
To be as these he loved in life and death.

And when his fading forces sank, there came
A band of helpers, priests and brethren true,
And ministering women, round his bed;
And there among his sick they labour still,
With others whom his bright example since
Inspired, lives dedicate like his to Heaven
And all the struggling suffering Race of men,
Working his work of mercy to the end.

Last, when, a year ago, his failing strength
Laid him upon his bed, keeping the use
Of his great Church, first would the good man make
Confession of his sins, and thanksgiving
Because the Lord had spared his life so long
To do his work. And round his dying bed
His people whom he succoured, a great throng
Of maimèd forms, swollen and scarred and bent
Out of all human semblance, came and wept,
And raised their poor hoarse voices in the hymns
He loved, and made a music dearer far
To the All-hearing Ear than any strain
Which skilful voices soaring to the vaults
Of dim cathedrals raise; and when at last,
After long weeks of suffering lit with prayer,
He gave his spirit back to God, and went
To be, at Easter, as he hoped, with Him
Who rose before, and the low passing-bell

Was heard, there went from that poor leprous throng
A solemn wailing, as from those who know
That they loved well and now had lost a friend."

Even as he ceased my soul within me leapt
In praise and thankfulness, and these her words:
"Ah! blessèd life which finds its happiness
In succouring others, with what store of good—
Good thoughts, good deeds, merciful energies—
Didst thou ascend to Heaven, and take thy rest!
I count not all, thy pangs of pain, or sense
Of natural loathing overcome by love,
Or the short years which brought their certain doom.
These, saintly lives lit by the sun of Faith,
Despise: but to know failure in thy work,
As thou didst oft; the souls which thou didst love
Unfaithful, and the hiss of slander mock
Thy purpose and thyself; to hear no voice
Of praise save that within thee sent from Heaven

Or some low faint applause of kindred souls,
Far off almost as from a separate star,
Whisper across the world, while the base din
Of loud detraction smote men's ears; to long
For home and feel thy own act banish thee,
And know inexorable Nature lurk
Behind thee, a deaf Fury pitiless,
Wielding a scourge of fire; to ask sometimes
In deep depression, as thy Master asked,
' Hast Thou forsaken me?' and find no voice
To answer thee, nor pity, nor reprieve
For all thy sacrifice, nor favouring word—
A martyrdom of years;—this were, indeed,
Too hard to bear for any but a soul
Fired as thine was, nay is, with love immense
As Heaven itself, stronger than Life or Death—
The love of God through weak and suffering man,
The love of man through his Creator, God."

But many a saintly form I knew, and passed
Without a word, because no vision long
Endures, and that for all no mortal life
Might well suffice. Did I not note thy fair
Nude youthful grace, Sebastian—beautiful
As young Apollo on the Olympian hill,
Or Marsyas, his victim—fettered fast
And pierced by rankling shafts while thou didst raise
Thy patient eyes to Heaven? Saw I not thee,
Oh sainted childlike Agnes, with thick locks
Of gold, which, grown miraculously long,
Guarded thy maiden modesty; or thee,
S. Agatha, with thy white wounded breast—
Martyrs and saints? Or thee of recent days,

S. Vincent, who thy late-enfranchised years,
Free from the prison bonds thou long hadst borne,
Didst spend in works of mercy, and didst care,
As might a father, for the childish lives
Forlorn which no man heeded? Saw I not
Thee, saintly Jeremy, whose daily feet
Paced 'neath the long-armed oaks of Golden Grove,
Above our winding Towy; or thy mild,
Benevolent gaze, good Howard, who didst die,
Christ-like, for souls in prison? Saw I not,
Blessing our land, thy apostolic form,
Dear Wesley, through whose white soul Love Divine
Shone unrefracted, whose pure life was full
Of love for God and man, whose faithful hand
Relit the expiring fire, which sloth and sense
And the sad world's unfaith had wellnigh quenched
And left in ashes; or thy saintly friend,
Fletcher of Madeley, clean consumed of faith
And ruth for perishing souls; or thee, whose zeal

Laid all thy learning at His feet who gave it,
Eliot, apostle to the dying race
Of the Red Indian, on their trackless plains
Preaching in their own tongue the gracious news
Thy learning opened; or thy comely form,
Brave Dorothy, who thy abounding life,
'Neath smoke-stained skies, 'mid coarse and brutal souls,
Gavest to the maimed and sick, content to be
A happy life-long martyr, and didst die
Alone at last of hopeless torture, pains
Incurable, yet cheerful barest thy cross
Even to the end; or ye, oh priceless lives!
After long years of terror, day and night,
Till death itself seemed better than your dread,
Shed for the Faith by many a savage isle
Of the Pacific seas; or ye whose graves
'Mid fever-swamps or silent forest depths
The Moslem slaver mocks, sent to sure death
For Africa. Nay, nay, I marked ye all,

But might not tarry more, so vast has grown,
Lost in dim eld, and longer, hour by hour,
The ever-lengthening pageant of the Blest.

And then there came no other name men know,
For now we passed along the close-set files
Of saints and martyrs, bearing each the palm,
Though marked no more by robes antique, or mien,
Or speech, but of the modern centuries,
And as we live to-day. So thick they rose
Streaming from earth, as when the autumnal year
Sheds its fair throng of meteors on the sky.
So those pure souls, white with a glittering train
Of light, flashed upward, till I might not take
Count of their number, for of every race
And hue and creed they came, of every age,
Both young and old—all to the heavens above
Rose upward; and an infinite thankfulness
Took me, and joy, because our day, that seems

To some so void of faith, so full of pain
And chilled with deadly doubt, not less than those
The faithful ages might, sent forth its tale
Of victories of the Faith.   Nor bore they all
The name of Christ, but some there were who held
The old unchanging Faith from whence He came
Whom yet their fathers slew, and some who called
On that ascetic Prince who draws the East
With some faint law of Mercy and of Love
For all created essences, one hope
To be with God, even though Man's nature rush
To His as doth the river to the sea,
Absorbed in Him for ever ; and of those
To whom the fierce false Prophet calling, taught,
Though stained with fanatic zeal and grovelling sense,
Amid the noise of base idolatries,
The unity of God, the pure, the wise,
Who sits to judge the world ; there came who left
The sensual stye and rose above the din

Of the world's wranglings, and who were indeed
His saints, though Him they knew not.

         But of all
The most part were of Him, each Christian race
Sending its cloud of witnesses to swell
The innumerable host. There, came the thralls
Of Duty, willing servants old and young,
Who kiss the chain that binds them, knowing well
That 'tis true freedom ; men who toil enchained
Of household care, knowing not rest nor ease,
For those they love, and live their briefer lives
For Duty ; or grave statesmen who toil on
To the laborious end, though life sink low,
Whom natural rest allures, but strive on still
While the sharp tooth of slander gnaws their souls.
Or women who have given their ease, their life,
To weary cares, nor heed them if they know
Their children happy ; or who from the hush
Of cloistered convents serve with prayer and praise ;

Or who amid the poor and lowly folk
Of all the Churches, as their Master erst,
Toil amid sin and pain, and are content
To live compassionate days and ask no more
Of wages for their service, but, consumed
Of pity, give their lives to save the lost
And hopeless; or who love to minister,
Spurning the weakness of their sex, the bloom
Of delicate ease, and grace and luxury,
And, 'mid the teeming homes of healing, bend
To succour bodily ill, while night by night
The sick and maimed, in restless slumbers tost,
Lie groaning till the dawn, and cries of pain
Wring the soft hearts whose duty binds them fast,
While the gay festive hearths of friends or home
Thrill with sweet music and the rhythmic feet
Of careless youth and joyance, and the rose
And lily of their gentle girlhood wait
Their coming, but in vain, till youth is past,

And with it earthly love.   All these fair souls
In one incessant effluence of light
Soared from the earth, the army of the saints
Who in all time have set themselves to work
The Eternal Will.

     And yet not all of pain
And suffering were they, that thus leaving earth,
Soared to high Heaven.   To some, high sacrifice
Is joy, not pain.   For some, from youth to age,
The even current of their lives flows on,
Broken by scarce a ripple, scarce a cloud
Veiling the constant blue—the daily use
Of humble duty, the unchanging round
Of homely life; the father's work, who toils
Ungrudging day by day, from year to year,
To keep the lives he loves, and dies too soon,
His children round his bed, nor knows at all
The tremours of the saint; the lowly tasks
Which fill the daily round of busy lives,

And keep them pure; the willing, cheerful care
Of mothers. Wert thou not among the throng,
Dear life long fled, who, after tranquil years
Unbroken and unclouded by great griefs
Or bodily pains, on the sad year's last day
Wentest from us; who threescore years and ten
Didst wear thy children's love; whose pitying hand
Was always open; whose mild voice and eye
Drew rich and poor alike, a love that soared
Not on great sacrifice, indeed, or high
And saintly pains, but trod life's level plain
As 'twere high snows, and daily did inform
Earth with some hue of Heaven; on whose loved tomb
No word is graven, save thy name and date
Of birth and death, because it seemed that none
Might fit the gracious life and beautiful,
Whose glory was its humbleness, whose work,
Built of sweet acts and precious courtesies,
The exemplar of a home? Nay, well I know

High Heaven were not Heaven, wanting thee
And such as thou.   Within the gates of God
Are many mansions, and each saintly soul
Treads its own path, fills its own place, but all
Are perfected and blest.
                        And yet how few
Of that great congress saw I.   He who spends
Lone vigils with the stars notes on night's face
Some ghostly, scarce-suspected vapour gleam,
And turns his optic-glass to it; and, lo!
A mist of suns! wherefrom the sensitive disc
Fixes the rays, first scattered, then more dense
With longer time, star after hidden star
Stealing from out the unimagined void
And twinkling into light, till on its face
Those dark unplumbed abysses show no speck
Of vacant gloom, a white and shining wall
Of glomerated worlds, broad as the bound
Which feeble fancy, yearning for an end,

Builds round the verge of Space. So that bright throng
Grew denser as I gazed, till Heaven was full
Of the white cloud of witnesses, who still,
As always since the worlds and Time began,
Stand round the throne of God.
      Then while I gazed,
As in that vision fair which filled the eyes
Of the blest seer of Patmos, suddenly
The angels with veiled faces cast them down
Prostrate, and then a peal of glorious sound,
Mightier than any sound of earth, which chased
My dream, and well-remembered words I heard:
" Blessing and Glory, Wisdom, Thanksgiving,
Honour, and Power, and Might be unto Thee
For ever and for ever."
      Then methought
My soul made answer:
      " Yea, and victory
Over Thy Evil. Not Thy saints alone

Are Thine, and if one soul were lost to Thee,
Thine arm were shortened.   All the myriad lives
Which are not here, but pine in bitter dole,
Do Thou redeem at last, after what toils
Thou wilt, in Thine own time, of Thine own will,
Purged, if Thou wilt, by age-long lustral pain,
Banished for long.   Yet through new spheres untried
Of Being let them rise, sinner and saint,
Higher and higher still, till all shall move
In harmony with Thee and Thy great Scheme,
Which doth transcend the bounds of Earth and Time ;
Still let them work Thy work.   Yet bring them home ;
Let none be lost !   For see how far thy Heavens
Are higher than our earth, how brief the tale
Of little years we live, how low and small
Our weak offence, transgression of a child
Grown petulant, on whom the father looks
With pity, not with wrath.   On those dead souls
Which unillumined in the outer depths

Lie yet, too gross for Heaven, send Thou a beam
From Thy great Sun, and, piercing through them, wake
The good that slept on earth : and, like the throb
Of radiant light which pulses through the mist
With which Thy Space is sown, and wakes new worlds,
Atom by atom drawn or else repelled ;
Or as the vibrant subtle note which thrills
Upon the sensitive film, and traces on it
Figure on figure, curve with curve inlaced
Into some flawless flower ; so do Thou, Lord,
Sound with Thy light and voice the dark dumb depths
And, working on the unnumbered souls which lie
Far from Thee, shine and call, and, waking in them
A latent order, purge them. Make their will
Harmonious with the Will which governs all,
And orb into some higher form, and start
As Thy new worlds to life, till all Thy skies

Shine with recovered souls. Then shall it be
As those great voices would, and Thou fulfilled
Alike in Earth and Heaven."

         But as I woke
To this poor world again, almost with tears,
Not wholly did the vision fade, but still
Those high processions lingering with me seemed
To purify my soul. What was the world,
Its low designs and hopes, its earth-born joys,
Base grovelling pleasures, and unfruitful pains,
To those and such as they—those eyes that saw
Not earth, but Heaven; those stainless feet that trod
Through lilied meads of saintly sacrifice
And strange unearthly snows? Surely 'twas well

To have seen them clearer than the mists of earth
Allow to waking hours. Come thou again,
Fair dream, and often, till thou art a dream
No more, but waking. March to victory,
Great army, from the legendary Past,
Through the brief Present, where Life's pilgrims toil
To-day, and rise triumphant, or fall prone,
Prest by their load ; through that unnoted tract
Of the dim Future which our thought pourtrays,
Far fairer than the world's sad Past; which yet
Shall have its struggles too, its sins, its wrongs,
Its saints, its martyrs !
      March in stainless line,
Lengthening the ranks of those who, gone before,
Are now triumphant, till the End shall come,
Which hushes all our lower strifes, attunes
Discords to harmonies, rounds and makes complete
The cycles of our Lives; till Sacrifice
And Pain are done, and Death, and the Dread Dawn

Breaks which makes all things new, and the great Sun
Rising upon the worlds, dispels the Night
Of Man's sad Past, and routs the gathered clouds
Of Evil, and ascends a Conqueror,
Wielding full splendours of unwaning Day
For ever!

THE END.

SELECTIONS FROM THE NOTICES

OF THE

POETICAL WORKS

OF

LEWIS MORRIS.

SONGS OF TWO WORLDS.

FIRST SERIES.

"The chief poem of the book is an allegory of the modern soul. It is like both an 'Odyssey' and a 'Faust,' but being within the compass of forty-four pages, of course runs chiefly over the surface of these vast problems and searching experiences. Yet it seizes the point of successive phases of the spirit's effort and craving in a remarkable way."—*Fortnightly Review*, July 15th, 1872.

"In 'The Wanderer,' the verse describing Socrates has that highest note of critical poetry, that in it epigram becomes vivid with life, and life reveals its inherent paradox. It would be difficult to describe the famous irony of Socrates in more poetical and more accurate words than by saying that he doubted men's doubts away."—*Spectator*, February 17th, 1872.

SECOND SERIES.

"In earnestness, sweetness, and the gift of depicting nature, the writer may be pronounced a worthy disciple of his compatriot, Henry Vaughan, the Silurist. Several of the shorter poems are instinct with a noble purpose and a high ideal of life. The most noteworthy poem is the 'Ode on a Fair Spring Morning,' which has somewhat of the charm and truth to nature of 'L'Allegro' and 'Il Penseroso.' It is the nearest approach to a master-piece in the volume."—*Saturday Review*, May 30th, 1874.

"This volume contains at least one poem of great originality, as well as many of much tenderness, sweetness, and beauty. 'The Organ-Boy' we have read again and again, with fresh pleasure on every reading. It is as exquisite a little poem as we have read for many a day."—*Spectator*, June 13th, 1874.

THIRD SERIES.

"Not unworthy of its predecessors. It presents the same command of metre and diction, the same contrasts of mood, the same grace and sweetness. It cannot be denied that he has won a definite position among contemporary poets."—*Times*, October 16th, 1875.

"'Evensong' shows power, thought, and courage to grapple with the profoundest problems. In the 'Ode to Free Rome' we find worthy treatment of the subject and passionate expression of generous sympathy."—*Saturday Review*, July 31st, 1875.

"More perfect in execution than either of its predecessors. . . . The pure lyrics are sweeter and richer. In the 'Birth of Verse' every stanza is a little poem in itself, and yet a part of a perfect whole."—*Spectator*, May 22nd, 1875.

THE EPIC OF HADES.

BOOK II.[*]

"Fresh, picturesque, and by no means deficient in intensity; but the most conspicuous merits of the author are the judgment and moderation with which his poem is designed, his self-possession within his prescribed limits, and the unfailing elegance of his

---

[*] Book II. was issued as a separate volume prior to the publication of Books I. and III. and of the complete work.

composition, which shrinks from obscurity, exuberance, and rash or painful effort as religiously as many recent poets seem to cultivate such interesting blemishes. . . ."—*Pall Mall Gazette*, March 10th, 1876.

"'Marsyas' is full of fine fancy and vivid description. His 'Andromeda' has to us one recommendation denied to Kingsley's —a more congenial metre; another is its unstrained and natural narrative."—*Saturday Review*, May 20th, 1876.

"The passage in which Apollo's victory over Marsyas and its effect are described is full of exquisite beauty. It is almost as fine as verse on such a subject could be. . . . From the first line to the last, the high and delicate aroma of purity breathes through the various spiritual fables."—*Spectator*, May 27th, 1876.

"The writer has shown himself more critical than his friends. . . . This long passage studded with graces."—*Academy*, April 29th, 1876.

BOOKS I. and III. and the COMPLETE WORK.

"Not only ambitious, but audacious, for it necessarily awakens reminiscences of Dante. Not unfrequently he is charmingly pathetic, as in his Helen and Psyche. There is considerable force and no small imagination in the description of some of the tortures in the 'Tartarus.' There is genuine poetical feeling in the 'Olympus.' . . . But it is more easy to give honest general praise than to single out particular extracts."—*Times*, February 9th, 1877.

"The whole of this last portion of the poem is exceedingly beautiful. . . . Nor will any, except critics of limited view, fail to recognize in the Epic a distinct addition to their store of those companions of whom we never grow tired."—*Athenæum*, March 3rd, 1877.

OPINIONS OF THE PRESS.

"One of the most considerable and original feats of recent English poetry."—*Saturday Review*, March 31st, 1877.

"Will live as a poem of permanent power and charm. It will receive high appreciation from all who can enter into its meaning, for its graphic and liquid pictures of external beauty, the depth and truth of its purgatorial ideas, and the ardour, tenderness, and exaltation of its spiritual life."—*Spectator*, May 5th, 1877.

"I have lately been reading a poem which has interested me very much, a poem called 'The Epic of Hades.' It is, as I view it, another gem added to the wealth of the poetry of our language."—*Mr. Bright's speech on Cobden, at Bradford*, July 25th, 1877.

"I have read the 'Epic of Hades,' and find it truly charming. Its pictures will long remain with me, and the music of its words."—OLIVER WENDELL HOLMES, April, 1884.

THE EPIC OF HADES.

ILLUSTRATED QUARTO EDITION.

"Of Mr. Chapman's illustrations it is pleasant to be able to speak with considerable admiration, not only because they are a fortunate echo of the verse, and represent the feelings and incidents of the 'Epic,' but because of their intrinsic merits. There is in them a fine and high inspiration of an indefinite sort."—*Athenæum*, March 29th, 1879.

"'The Epic of Hades' is certainly one of the most remarkable works of the latter half of the nineteenth century. Here is an *édition de luxe* which may possibly tempt the unthinking to search for the jewel within the casket."—*World*, February 12th, 1879.

"The author has been most fortunate in his illustrator. The designs are gems of drawing and conception, and the mezzotint is admirably adapted to the style of drawing and subject."—*Art Journal*, April, 1879.

"'The Epic of Hades' has already won a place among the immortals. These designs are noteworthy for their tenderness of sentiment and their languid grace."—*Daily News*, April 2nd, 1879.

GWEN:

A DRAMA IN MONOLOGUE.

"The charm of this beautiful little poem is its perfect simplicity of utterance; its chastened and exquisite grace. The genius of the author has closed an idyll of love and death with a strain of sweet, sad music in that minor key which belongs to remembrance and regret."—*Daily News*, January 22nd, 1879.

"Few among the later poets of our time have received such a generous welcome as the author. He has been appreciated not by critics alone, but by the general public. . . . The charm of 'Gwen' is to be found in the limpid clearness of the versification, in the pathetic notes which tell the old story of true love wounded and crushed."—*Pall Mall Gazette*, October 8th, 1879.

"The writer has gained inspiration from themes which inspired Dante; he has sung sweet songs and musical lyrics; and whether writing in rhyme or blank verse, has proved himself a master of his instrument."—*Spectator*, July 26th, 1879.

THE ODE OF LIFE.

"The 'Ode of Life' ought to be the most popular of all the author's works. People flock to hear great preachers, but in this book they will hear a voice more eloquent than theirs, dealing with the most important subjects that can ever occupy the thoughts of man."—*Westminster Review*, July, 1880.

"The author is one of the few real poets now living. Anything at once more sympathetic and powerful it would be difficult to find in the poetry of the present day."—*Scotsman*, May 11th, 1880.

"A high devout purpose and wide human sympathy ennoble all the writer's work, and his clear language and quiet music will retain his audience."—*Nineteenth Century*, August, 1880.

"Any notice of recent poetry would be inadequate without a reference to the 'Ode of Life.' The only fault we have to find with this really remarkable effort—a sort of expansion of Wordsworth's famous Ode—is that it is rather too long for its ideas; but it possesses power, sweetness, occasional profundity, and unmistakable music."—*Contemporary Review*, February, 1881.

SONGS UNSUNG.

"Some of the more important pieces make almost equal and very high demands alike on my sympathy and my admiration."—Mr. GLADSTONE, November, 1883.

"The reader of his former work will probably commence this volume with considerable expectations. Nor will he be altogether disappointed, although he will probably wish that Mr. Morris had given the world more of his exquisite classical workmanship."—*Fortnightly Review*, November, 1883.

"'The New Creed' is, in some respects, his most striking achievement. The poem is one well suited to his mind, but we are not aware that he has ever before written anything at once so impressive, so solemn, and so self-restrained. The last two lines have all the happy energy of the highest poetry."—*Spectator*, November 10th, 1883.

"In reading it one feels constantly 'How worthy this book would be of beautiful illustrations!'"—*Academy*, November 24th, 1883.

"For ourselves we dare hardly say how high we rank Mr. Morris. This last volume is deserving of highest praise. In some of its contents no living poet, to our mind, can surpass him."—*Oxford University Herald*, March 8th, 1884.

"In one sense 'Songs Unsung' is more typical of Mr. Morris's genius than any of his previous works. There is in them the same purity of expression, the same delicate fancy, the same mastery of technique, and withal the same loftiness of conception."—*Scotsman*, December 22nd, 1883.

"In some respects we must award him the distinction of having a clearer perception of the springs of nineteenth-century existence than any of his contemporaries. . . . What could be more magnificent than the following conception of the beginning of things. . . ."—*Whitehall Review*, October, 1883.

"We have quoted enough to show that this book has genuine merit in it, merit in poetry, merit in philosophy, and, we may add, merit in religion. There are living poets greater than Lewis Morris, but of the younger race of poets he is foremost."—*The Inquirer*, April 5th, 1884.

""This volume is likely to add to his reputation. It is healthy in tone, and shows no decline of the varied qualities to which the author owes his widespread reputation."—*Times*, June 9, 1884.

GYCIA.

"' Gycia' abounds in powerful dramatic situations, while the intricate evolutions of a double plot in love and statecraft provoke perpetual curiosity, which is only fully satisfied at the end. The heroine, in her single-minded patriotism and her undeviating devotion to duty, rises to the level of the loftiest feminine conceptions of the old Greek dramatists. And she is finely contrasted with her generous and impulsive husband, who has neither her sternness of principle nor her steadiness of purpose. The form of the verse is so picturesque, and the flow is so free, that we should say, if effectively delivered, it must command an appreciative audience. It would have been difficult for any poet to do full justice to the thrilling scene where Gycia denounces the treason of her husband and his countrymen to the chief magistrates of the State. Yet Mr. Morris has done it well. Nearly as stirring, and even more pathetic, is the scene where the pair are seated side by side in state, with anguished hearts and smiling faces, at the banquet, which, as each knows well, is to end with a horrible catastrophe."—*Times*, October 18th, 1886.

"The *dramatis personae* have life and individuality; the situations are for the most part strong and rich in really dramatic effects; the architecture of the plot is simple, harmonious, and symmetrical, without any of that obtrusive artificiality which often accompanies symmetry; and the action never drags, but is always in determinate progressive movement. A drama of which these things can be truthfully said is not merely good as drama, but has that element of popularity which is of more practical value than the absolute goodness of which only critics take account. The verse is, throughout, strong, fluent, rich, variously expressive, and adequate with that adequacy which satisfies without drawing attention to itself."—MR. J. A. NOBLE, *in the Academy*, November 20th, 1886.

"Throughout there is the artistic contrast and striving between the spirit of liberty and tyranny, between Republican simplicity and patrician form and ceremony, and a great political lesson is taught. It is hardly necessary to praise the nobility and the dignity, the sweetness and the strength, of Mr. Morris's verse. 'Gycia' will add to his already firmly founded reputation as a dramatic poet and writer of noble blank verse. It is one of the few works by recent English poets that seem capable of thrilling an audience upon the stage, as well as enchaining the mind of the student in the chamber."—*Scotsman*, November 10th, 1886.

"I have lost no time in reading your tragedy. I perused it with great interest, and a sense throughout of its high poetic powers."—MR. GLADSTONE, October 20th, 1886.

"Notwithstanding all drawbacks, we think that 'Gycia' is by very much the best contribution that Mr. Morris has yet made to literature. It is full of solid work, and has a strong current of interest. It might be remodelled into a very fine stage play."—*Liverpool Mercury*, November 8th, 1886.

"Want of space prevents us from entering into any close criticism, and also from giving specimens of passages of poetic merit in which Mr. Morris has done himself justice, and which will be read with pleasure. Such passages are plentiful in 'Gycia.'"—*Athenæum*, December 18th, 1886.

"To take up 'Gycia' is not to lay it aside again until you have read it through to the last page. It possesses all the requisites for a good play. Whether it succeed on the stage or not, and we heartily wish it success, it will ever be read with pleasure by those who can appreciate what there is of refined and beautiful, noble and true in literature, or art, or higher things still."—*The Month*, January, 1887.

"In its tragic ending, mournful though it is, there is true poetic justice, and no one can close the book without having been interested and often touched and thrilled by the true magic of the poetic spell."—*Anglican Church Magazine*.

SONGS OF BRITAIN.

"Mr. Morris has done well to incorporate in his new volume three stories of Wild Wales, which are its most important portion. They are told with spirit and charm of local colour. In his treatment of subjects already free of Parnassus, he has a happy way of hitting off charming pictures and felicitous modes of expression."—*Athenæum*, April 30th, 1887.

"Mr. Morris's new book strikes us as being by much the most popular that he has yet put forth, and its most popular portions are the poems founded on old Welsh peasant tradition. 'Llyn y Morwynion' is a beautiful legend of love and death. But by far the most beautiful of these legends of Wild Wales is that which he calls 'The Physicians of Myddfai.' In telling these legends, Mr. Morris displays greater poetic quality than he has ever before shown. His verse is richer, fuller, and more melodious, but, better than this, his feeling for his subject is well-nigh perfect. Such lightness of touch and such sympathy he has never before shown. It is easy to mar the exquisite beauty of such gossamer things as these old traditions, but he has not done so by so much as a jarring word. Softly, sweetly, tenderly, the story glides along, and not until the last word is reached is the spell broken. Mr. Morris has here cut his highest niche as a poet."—*Liverpool Mercury*, April 30th, 1887.

"Upon these beautiful Welsh poems we very heartily congratulate Mr. Morris. If Wales has many more such entrancing stories as these to tell, he may find his surest title to lasting fame in marrying them to melodious verse."—*Liverpool Daily Post*, May 16th, 1887.

"Mr. Lewis Morris gained his place years ago in the higher rank of contemporary poets. In the preludes to these romantic tales he sketches both tenderly and truthfully the present aspects of local scenery, and the manners of the Welsh people. But the finest piece in this volume is one belonging to Greater Britain, 'A Song of Empire for the Queen's Jubilee Year.' It merits to be the inaugural ode of the Imperial Institute."—*Illustrated News*, May 14th, 1887.

"Mr. Morris's new volume exhibits those qualities to which are due his well-earned distinction and widespread popularity. Choice and dainty language, good taste, natural feeling, not passionately strong, indeed, but sincere and unaffected, and a considerable sense of beauty make his writing generally good reading, and do not fail us in this instance."—*Christian World*, April 28th, 1887.

"Mr. Morris is not a profound thinker, nor has he anything very momentous to say which we have not heard long ago. As to technical form and diction, his fame will rest on his blank verse, which is remarkably lucid, even, and sustained, often powerful, and sometimes highly beautiful. He composes fine pictures, and paints them well and strongly with a certain mannerism—the manner of Tennyson at his best. In the beautiful poem, 'In Pembrokeshire, 1886,' and elsewhere, he gives us the perfect atmosphere and sentiment of scenery, but then so many of the moderns have caught this art."—*Pall Mall Gazette*, May 23rd, 1887.

"Delicacy of feeling and a deep sense of the beauty of nature characterize these poems. Those inspired by 'Wild

Wales' are remarkable for lyrical strength and vivid descriptive power."—*Morning Post*, May 2nd, 1887.

"This charming volume, . . . while it fails to augment to any appreciable degree its author's fame, worthily sustains the poetic reputation which he has so honourably won."—*Leeds Mercury*, May 31st, 1887.

"The most striking poems in the volume, rising highest in purpose and sustained with intellectual force and imaginative energy, are the three that embody legends of Wild Wales. Here Mr. Morris has struck a prolific and valuable vein. . . . His poetic discrimination, suggestive observant bias, delight in rural scenery, elevation of purpose, and strong moral sense are all here as of old. . . . A volume that all lovers of poetry will cherish as a precious possession."—*Scottish News*, June 14th, 1887.

"These lines are quite up to the standard of the 'Epic of Hades,' and it would be hard to find anywhere a more beautiful image than that of the 'white birds swooping down.'"—*Literary World*, June 16th, 1887.

www.ingramcontent.com/pod-product-compliance
Lightning Source LLC
Chambersburg PA
CBHW030740230426
43667CB00007B/789